Forgiveness and the Healing Process

Many people come for help because they remain stuck in a destructive relationship, job, legal battle or memories of child abuse. A growing number of therapists believe that forgiveness is of crucial importance in helping people break away from these patterns of resentment and revenge.

Does forgiveness help? Or is the concept out of date in our more secular society? *Forgiveness and the Healing Process* considers this debate. Experienced contributors:

- Consider the place of forgiveness in working with individuals and couples.
- Explore the benefits of mediation as a way forward for both the individual and the organisation, and also within the criminal justice system.
- Offer a valuable insight into South Africa's Truth and Reconciliation Commission and the crucial role of forgiveness in post-apartheid South Africa.
- Examine a client's view of developing the capacity to forgive.
- Present new frameworks for workers seeking to help people cope with trauma and injustice.

Forgiveness and the Healing Process helps counsellors, psychotherapists, social workers, mediators, psychiatrists, and those working in the criminal justice system understand how forgiveness can facilitate the therapeutic process.

Cynthia Ransley is a lecturer and course leader in social work at Brunel University. She is an integrative psychotherapist, supervisor and trainer in London.

Terri Spy is a counselling psychologist and fellow of the British Association for Counselling and Psychotherapy. She is a London-based integrative psychotherapist, supervisor and trainer.

'A very welcome and timely contribution to a field often dominated by psychological categories, this book adds to the interdisciplinary base of counselling and psychotherapy, to the skills and capacity of practitioners and to our understanding generally of the place of forgiveness in healing our wounds: violence, war, crime, sexual abuse, racism, interpersonal conflict. The editors have assembled a team of excellent writers and subtle arguments. Contemporary, accessible, theoretically authoritative and practically informative, *Forgiveness and the Healing Process* embraces the political, theological, criminological, organisational and psychotherapeutic dimensions and dynamics of forgiveness and reconciliation in a way no other book does. An increasingly dangerous world needs such ideas to interrupt the cycles of hurt, blame, stalemate and revenge. Above all, readers, whether "religious" or not, will be stimulated by the mosaic of perspectives offered here.'

Colin Feltham, Reader in Counselling,
Sheffield Hallam University, UK

Forgiveness and the Healing Process

A central therapeutic concern

Edited by
Cynthia Ransley and Terri Spy

Brunner-Routledge
Taylor & Francis Group

HOVE AND NEW YORK

First published 2004
by Brunner-Routledge
27 Church Road, Hove, East Sussex BN3 2FA

Simultaneously published in the USA and Canada
by Brunner-Routledge
29 West 35th Street, New York NY 10001

Brunner-Routledge is an imprint of the Taylor & Francis Group

Typeset in Times by Mayhew Typesetting, Rhayader, Powys
Printed and bound in Great Britain by TJ International, Padstow, Cornwall
Paperback cover design by Anú Design

British Library Cataloguing in Publication Data
A catalogue record for this book is available from the British Library

Library of Congress Cataloging-in-Publication Data
Forgiveness and the healing process : a central therapeutic concern /
[edited by] Cynthia Ransley and Terri Spy.
         p. cm.
Includes bibliographical references and index.
    ISBN 1-58391-182-0 (alk. paper) – ISBN 1-58391-183-9 (pbk. : alk.
paper)
1. Forgiveness. 2. Forgiveness–Therapeutic use. 3.
Forgiveness–Religious aspects. I. Ransley, Cynthia. II. Spy, Terri.

   BF637 F67F66 2003
   155.9'2–dc21

                                                        2003011790

ISBN 1-58391-182-0 (hbk)
ISBN 1-58391-183-9 (pbk)

For the many people who struggle with the concept of forgiveness.

(TS)

For my parents, Mary and Mendel Harris, with love.

(CR)

Contents

Notes on contributors

Michael Carroll Phd is a fellow of the British Association for Counselling and Psychotherapy, a chartered counselling psychologist and a British Association for Counselling and Psychotherapy (BACP) Senior Registered Practitioner. He works as a counsellor, supervisor, trainer and consultant to organisations in both public and private sectors, specialising in the area of employee well-being. He has lectured and trained both nationally and internationally. Michael is Visiting Industrial Professor in the Graduate School of Education, University of Bristol and the winner of the 2001 British Psychological Society Award for Distinguished Contributions to Professional Psychology.

He has written and edited a number of key texts on supervision and counselling including *Integrative Approaches to Supervision* (edited with Margaret Tholstrup, Jessica Kingsley 2001), *The Handbook of Counselling in Organisations* (edited with Michael Walton, Sage 1997) and *Workplace Counselling* (Sage 1996).

Jane Cooper qualified as a doctor from St Bartholomew's Hospital in 1979. She undertook training with the Institute of Psychosexual Medicine under Tom Main, gaining membership in 1992. She then trained as a Gestalt psychotherapist at the Sherwood Psychotherapy Institute, under Ken Evans, gaining the diploma in 1998. She now works part time in the National Health Service in genito-urinary medicine and runs a private psychotherapy and supervision practice in Surrey for individuals and couples.

Gill Eagle is a registered clinical psychologist, Associate Professor at the University of the Witwatersrand in South Africa and member of the board of, and consultant to, the Centre for the Study of Violence and Reconciliation. She has worked in the field of traumatic stress studies for almost 20 years with a focus on critical understandings of violence and its impact. She has researched, intervened and consulted in the areas of sexual violence, civil conflict and criminal violence among others. She has a special interest in the social location of victims, including the dynamic role played by gender, culture and class-related factors. She has published several articles in the field and given numerous conference presentations.

Maria Gilbert MA (Clin Psych) is a chartered clinical psychologist and United Kingdom Council for Psychotherapy (UKCP) registered integrative psychotherapist. She is currently head of the Integrative Department (Psychotherapy and Counselling Psychology) at the Metanoia Institute in West London. She has a private practice as a psychotherapist, supervisor, consultant and trainer. Maria is the co-author with Kenneth Evans of the book *Psychotherapy Supervision: An Integrative Relational Approach* (Open University Press 2000) and, with Diana Shmukler, *Brief Therapy with Couples: An Integrative Approach* (John Wiley & Sons 1996).

Joy Green (not her real name) originally trained as a nursery nurse. After working as a residential nanny, she moved into training student nursery nurses. For many years, she worked as matron in residential homes with children who had been abused or had multiple disabilities. Joy trained as a social worker and then moved into adoption and fostering. Before retiring, she became a practice teacher for social work students. Joy is a practising Christian and is involved in pastoral care in her church.

Guy Masters has worked in the field of restorative justice since 1993. In 1998 Guy completed a PhD thesis in restorative justice and criminological theory at Lancaster University. He has since held a variety of positions as a researcher, policy adviser, practitioner and project developer. Most recently, he has worked for the Essex Family Group Conferencing Service, and is currently Referral Order Co-ordinator for Wandsworth Youth Offending Team. Guy wrote the majority of his chapter while a Research Fellow at the Australian National University.

Fathima Moosa is a clinical psychologist currently residing in Sydney, Australia. She was previously a lecturer in the Department of Psychology at the University of the Witwatersrand in South Africa. She worked in South Africa with survivors of psychological torture and trauma. She is currently working as a clinical psychologist at Encompass Australasia, an organisation that offers counselling services to professionals (including individuals engaged in ministry) who are struggling with issues of boundary violations as well as other psychological difficulties.

Cynthia Ransley MSc originally trained as a social worker. She now works part-time at Brunel University, Middlesex where she is the course leader of a social work programme. She trained as an integrative psychotherapist at the Metanoia Institute where she is a tutor. She has a private practice in West London as a psychotherapist, supervisor and trainer. Twenty years ago, Cynthia was a founder and is currently a trustee of a charity, Action for the Victims of Medical Accidents. Her publications include *Developing your Learning Skills* (BASW/Open Learning Foundation 1996).

Terri Spy MSc is a counselling psychologist and Fellow of the British Association of Counselling and Psychotherapy (BACP). Terri is accredited by BACP as a counsellor, supervisor and trainer. She is also a United Kingdom Council for Psychotherapy (UKCP) registered integrative psychotherapist. Terri, as a practising Christian, has a commitment to equality of people regardless of race, culture, gender or ability. She is involved with several organisations which provide training, conferences, and counselling advice. Publications include 'Supervision and Working with Disability' (with Caron Oyston) in *Counselling, Supervision and Context* (Sage 1999).

Gill Straker is a clinical psychologist currently residing in Sydney, Australia, where she has a private psychotherapy and supervision practice. She previously occupied the Chair of Applied Psychology at the University of the Witwatersrand in South Africa. She worked with township youth in South Africa who were engaged in the country's liberation struggle, as well as with other survivors of psychological torture and trauma. She is currently Clinical Professor of Psychology at the University of Sydney. She also serves as consultant to Encompass Australasia.

Foreword

How we construct meaning comes from our own background and history, unique constitution and interface with others. In training as therapists we undertake our own psychotherapy, counselling or psychoanalysis. We hope to understand others better through understanding ourselves more. We now consider issues around social class, gender and race. However, how much do we consider religious difference in our tolerant western society?

Coming from an agnostic Jewish background I was moved by the words of a deeply religious abuse survivor: 'It hurt me to have heard you describe yourself as agnostic. How will you understand my religious experiences that are so life-saving to me? In order to go to someone to share something of my pain, must I also face another area of my life not being shared?'

This book, co-edited by a committed Christian in Terri Spy and an agnostic in Cynthia Ransley, both distinguished integrative psychotherapists, allows such painful dilemmas and differences to be faced. Indeed, it was the request of a Christian patient who wished to forgive her parents for childhood abuse that led the agnostic Ransley to discuss the term 'forgiveness' with the Christian Terri Spy, who saw it as an integral part of the therapeutic process. An impressive range of other sources and religious beliefs also inform the book.

This book comes from the quest of one brave client, 'Charlotte' and includes the journey of another, 'Joy'. It includes the lived experience of the fine group of writers/thinkers/practitioners gathered here. It is a rare source book, a wake-up book and an invigorating and moving read.

Valerie Sinason

Acknowledgements

We would like to start by offering our sincere thanks to our contributors who took time out of their busy lives to set out their thoughts on forgiveness and offer valuable insights on their work.

So many people have encouraged us and offered their ideas on forgiveness while we were writing and editing this book – colleagues, friends, social work students, trainee therapists – and we want to thank them all. Cynthia wants to express her appreciation to all those who completed her questionnaire and provided such an interesting range of thoughts on forgiveness. And we want to acknowledge the help our clients have given us in developing our thinking and views.

A number of people have read and offered helpful comments on parts of the book. Here we would like to thank Graz Kowszun, Daphne Norden, Eileen Smith, Judy Scott, Inge Koopmans, Cecilia Frend and Ann Harvey. However, we would particularly like to acknowledge the help of Peter Ransley who read and reread our chapters and gave invaluable advice, encouragement, even food.

Finally, Cynthia would like to thank Peter, Nicholas and Bex for their support and for putting up with her endless preoccupation with a word they had hardly thought of before. And Terri would like to thank the Lord God, Inge and Jake for keeping her aware that there is more to life than books.

Introduction

Cynthia Ransley and Terri Spy

A woman phoned one of the editors, Cynthia Ransley, to explore having therapy. Charlotte (not her real name) explained that religion was important to her and asked Ransley whether she was a Christian. Though she said no, Charlotte decided to meet her. At the first session, she stated her goal and this was the seed from which this book has grown.

Charlotte said that what she wanted was to find a way to forgive her parents for the abuse she had suffered as a child. This took Ransley by surprise. No one had ever raised forgiveness as a goal with her before. An agnostic, she had always had something of an antipathy towards the term 'forgiveness', considering it rather patronising and value laden, like 'charity' and 'tolerance'. She talked about it with Terri Spy, another integrative psychotherapist, knowing that as a practising Christian Spy saw forgiveness as an integral part of the therapeutic process.

It was immediately obvious how often clients talked about forgiveness with Spy and how rarely it came up in Ransley's practice. What was not clear was how far this was connected with religious beliefs. Spy is explicit about her Christian beliefs. Some clients are drawn to her because of her faith, although the majority are not practising Christians. Ransley does not offer information about her beliefs and the client mentioned above was one of the few to ask. How much do our different value bases influence both what the client brings to the psychotherapy process and what do we as therapists tune into and miss? (Certainly the word 'forgiveness' has come up more often in Ransley's practice since she became involved in this book!) This question led to others. How aware are therapists of these issues? To what extent is forgiveness seen as a therapeutic goal?

Researching this, we found that none of the mainstream psychotherapeutic models of loss and change address the concept of forgiveness. There are religious books on the subject, but no UK counselling or psychotherapy book on forgiveness. It rarely, if ever, comes up in therapy training courses. Apart from Ken Hart and David Shapiro's work with recovering alcoholics at Leeds University, little research is being carried out in the UK on forgiveness therapy. We wondered, given the more secular nature of British society, whether other terms, such as 'acceptance' and 'reconciliation', tend to be used instead and, if so, whether they have similar connotations.

In America, it is a different story. There is an increasing amount of research being undertaken on forgiveness. A number of psychological books have been published in the field. Most have, as a starting point, a belief in the importance of forgiveness for good mental health and questions are being asked about whether there is a link between forgiveness and physical health. The contrast between the USA and the UK is stark. Does it stem from stronger religious movements in the USA, or simply the size of the population? Recent surveys give similar percentages of people stating they have a religious identification. Eighty-one per cent of Americans identified themselves with a religious group (Kosmin *et al.* 2001), while the 2001 British census gave the UK figure as just over 75 per cent. The important issue is the strength of commitment to a religious faith and it is difficult to obtain figures on this. Certainly the political and media influence of Christian groups in America suggests there is a deeper level of religion in the USA, particularly in the South. It is also worth noting the contrast between the UK population census and Ransley's albeit small-scale research among British therapists (Chapter 3) where only 42 per cent stated they had a religious affiliation.

People seek help for many different reasons. Some have been neglected in childhood and perhaps sexually or physically abused. Others have been on the receiving end of a traumatic wrongdoing, such as rape or fraud. Many people, because of their religious beliefs or personal philosophy, consider forgiving the other person crucial if they are to let go of a wrong and move on. And surely forgiving ourselves, developing our capacity to accept our own limitations and mistakes, is basic to our well-being, whatever the words we use to describe the process?

Forgiveness is at one and the same time an individual and a political or cultural phenomenon. You cannot watch a news programme or open a newspaper without being faced by a disaster or atrocity – a rail crash, murder, war. Particularly, since 11 September 2001 in New York, there has been a preoccupation with terrorism. How to respond? First, talk seems more often of revenge than forgiveness: 'an eye for an eye': '. . . the FBI investigates hate crimes against 40 US Muslims' (*Washington Post*, 18 September 2001); 'Pakistani mourners swear revenge on US . . . at the funeral of a leading pro-Taliban militant killed in a United States air raid on Kabul' (BBC, 25 October 2001). There have been numerous headlines in 2003 such as, 'Israel takes revenge by assassinating Hamas leader' (*Independent*, 22 August 2003); 'Palestinians vow revenge as they bury Hamas leader' (*Independent*, 23 August 2003).

There are more moderate headlines, talk of the need for a measured response, for bringing the person to justice – not revenge – after a brutal incident. But the line between justice and revenge is a narrow one: what is perceived as a measured response by one side may well be seen as retaliation by the other. The potential for violence to escalate is always there.

A few people can offer forgiveness without even an expression of remorse from the killers, indeed where it is likely that the perpetrator feels no remorse. Just after his daughter died in the Enniskillen bombing of 1987 in Ireland, Gordon Wilson forgave the killers: 'I bear no ill will. I bear no grudge . . . that will not bring her back . . . Whether or not they are judged here on earth by a court of law . . . I do my very best to show forgiveness . . . the last words rest with God' (Arnold 1998: 22). His plea was not a political one but a heartfelt hope that some good could come from his daughter's death. Is it easier to forgive when you have a God who will judge? Certainly Wilson's words stemmed, at least briefly, the cycle of killing and revenge in Ireland.

In 2002, a Palestinian, Ismail Hawaja showed a similar reaction when his wife was killed in their refugee camp home by Israeli soldiers. The *Christian Science Monitor* (March 2002) had the headline, 'A Widower offers Forgiveness in a Land of Vengeance'. They wrote that with more than a thousand Palestinians killed in the previous 18 months (and several hundred Israelis), voices of Palestinian or Israeli pacifists had been rare. Hawaja was firm: 'I have no grudges. The most important point is that my wife has been killed in front of her five children. I don't want this to happen to an Israeli'. A teacher, he had spent his life in refugee camps and the misery had brought him to the conclusion that peace was the only solution and violence could never be the means to peace.

The final example is of a murder, unrelated to war. Damilola Taylor, aged 12, bled to death in 2000 in London, after being attacked on his way home from school. The young men eventually accused of his murder were found not guilty. No one was sentenced for his death. There was no justice, yet Mr Taylor said he would pray for his son's killers. On the BBC's *HARDtalk*, he said that if he met them, 'I would ask them why did they did it – and if they are able to tell me and (if I could) feel their remorse, I would forgive them . . . We want them to be positive in life, walk towards a better future rather than being destructive . . .' (14 May 2002). The family have set up the Damilola Trust to support disadvantaged young people in the area.

Are seeking revenge and offering forgiveness two sides of the same coin, different ways of trying to take some control where there is such a despairing level of powerlessness? The ability to say 'I have no grudges' shows some understanding of the other side and, in the examples in Ireland and Palestine, an awareness that both sides have blood on their hands and must reconcile. For the Taylor family, there is hopefully some comfort from working towards prevention: the belief that the only way to try and prevent tragic murders in the future is to support youngsters who are disaffected and disadvantaged in our society.

Apologies, on the other hand, often seem a long time coming. It took 30 years for the IRA to apologise to the victims of the 'bloody Friday' violence in Belfast in 1972. It took even longer – two centuries – for the Dutch Queen Beatrix to unveil a slavery memorial, following an expression of remorse by her government for the country's part in the slave trade. This type of political apology often reopens the wound. 'Too little, too late' was how one victim of IRA violence reacted. The National Committee on Slavery demanded Queen Beatrix herself apologise and that the government pay reparations.

These reactions are reminiscent of the *Washington Post*'s headline after President Clinton's apology for lying about his sexual relationship with Monica Lewinsky: 'Mea Not So Culpa' (19 August 1998). People want sincere apologies and, increasingly, compensation as reparation for the offence committed. The increase in legal claims against doctors in the UK over the last 20 years, is one example.

Sometimes an apology is linked to a request for forgiveness. In a two-week period on the BBC news – apart from the apologies from the IRA and Queen Beatrix above – the Roman Catholic Church in New Zealand apologised to victims of sexual abuse, the Pope apologised to China for missionary activities and various UK government ministers apologised for mistakes such as pension blunders. The Catholic Church both apologised *and* asked for forgiveness. The government ministers in Britain did not ask the public for forgiveness, yet the German president begged Israel's forgiveness for the Holocaust.

Why do some people or institutions ask for forgiveness while others focus on the offering of an apology? Is this related to culture or religious faith? Is it related to the severity of the crime or how long ago it took place? Is the motivation the desire to reconcile, to enter into a positive relationship with the other party? These are some of the questions we will attempt to answer in this book.

A note of caution. Words such as 'forgiveness' have different connotations in different languages, cultures and religions – indeed some religions, like Buddhism, have no word at all for forgiveness. Look again at the headline about the Palestinian, Ismail Hawaja whose wife was killed by Israeli soldiers: 'A Widower offers Forgiveness'. From reading the detail in the article, one can see that he did not in fact use the term. The translation in the article was 'I have no grudges'. The word 'forgiveness' in the *Christian Science Monitor* headline, was *their* summary of what he said based on *their* cultural perspective, *their* use of language – prejudice if you like – which may or may not have been true to the nuance of his meaning. Language has power and in a world where bias is hard to avoid, it is clearly important that therapists check the precise meaning clients give to such words. It is their words, their meanings that matter.

The headlines quoted above identify people looking for revenge or letting go of grudges and offering forgiveness. In none of the cases do we know any detail of the struggle the people experienced, the range of feelings that they faced: fury, distress, powerlessness, empathy for the other. No one can begin to come to terms with what has happened without experiencing a whole spectrum of emotions. Premature desire to forgive can be just as debilitating as being stuck with the need for revenge.

Focus of the book

The editors' interest in bringing together a book on forgiveness stemmed from their differences. Unlike other books in the field, we wanted one which would highlight different perspectives on forgiveness and how this relates to practice. We were interested in whether issues varied in different contexts and with different client groups. Many of the contributors to the book offer both a perspective on forgiveness and a valuable insight into their area of practice based on years of experience as a practitioner or researcher.

Above all, we were interested in a book which would span the personal, professional and theoretical. We believe that personal issues are inextricably linked to the social and political context. In terms of political trauma and forgiveness, nowhere can this be seen more clearly than in South Africa with the Truth and Reconciliation Commission (TRC) and we are pleased to include a chapter from three South African therapists, Moosa, Straker and Eagle. The reader will find that some chapters, notably Green's account of her own journey to forgiveness, offer a personal perspective. Other chapters focus more on research and theory. Most of the contributions, as we have said, centre on therapeutic practice in a particular context. We are mindful that many professional groups work with people who have been traumatised by a wrongdoing. Our aim is a book which will be useful to a range of practitioners including therapists, health professionals, social workers, human resource managers, mediators and victim support workers.

The word 'wrongdoing' may need some explanation. We use the term to mean any unjust behaviour or misuse of power that is experienced or perceived as harmful. The scale of the wrong may be vastly different: genocide, political torture, sexual abuse, crime, domestic violence, negligence, infidelity, neglect. However, as Masters points out in relation to criminal offences (Chapter 6), the traumatic impact of the wrong does not necessarily reflect the scale of it.

We make no claims to be comprehensive and write as practitioners not philosophers or theologians. We have been inevitably limited by space in our ability to include perspectives from practitioners from different faith beliefs and from therapeutic approaches in which forgiveness is differently conceived. Hopefully the book will encourage others to contribute to the debate in the future. Meantime, we hope that readers will be challenged by our different perspectives to explore their own attitudes towards forgiveness and question their approach to helping a person traumatised by a wrongdoing.

In Chapter 1, Cynthia Ransley offers an overview of some of the themes addressed in the literature on forgiveness, almost all of which stems from the USA. She discusses the religious roots of the term, drawing on the five main western and eastern faith traditions. While many readers may associate forgiveness with Christianity, all the main faiths place value on the term, or allied concepts such as mercy and compassion. Ransley explores the diversity of meanings given to forgiveness in the literature and why it is seen as important. Finally she addresses the question of how people learn and can be helped, by therapy and education, to forgive.

In Chapter 2, Terri Spy offers a personal perspective of her work as a therapist who is a practising Christian. She discusses her value base, which firmly rests on the Bible and various Christian thinkers. Working with forgiveness is central to her approach and she explores some of the differences in her work with practising Christians and non-Christians. She offers a framework for working with clients on forgiveness, which she sees as equally useful in helping people move towards reconciliation or acceptance.

Chapter 3 offers a different point of view. In 'Be cautious about forgiveness', Cynthia Ransley warns readers to tread carefully about the use of the term 'forgiveness' and the motivation behind it. She bases this on research she undertook with more than 100 therapists and social workers. Opinions were diverse: for some, forgiveness was a crucial value in their lives, for others the word had negative connotations. She explores the link between power and forgiveness and warns of the potential for people to forgive from a position of superiority as well as for people to feel coerced by moral principles to forgive.

In Chapter 4, Jane Cooper and Maria Gilbert explore 'The role of forgiveness in working with couples'. They hold the view that forgiveness can only truly take place when both parties actively seek and welcome it; when the depth of hurt has been fully experienced by both parties and reparations made. They see forgiveness as dependent on people's capacity for empathy and ability to enter into the experience of the other person while remaining grounded in their own. They set out a process model of forgiveness for work with couples and linked to case examples from their practice.

While many of the chapters focus primarily on therapist and client, in Chapter 5 Michael Carroll offers a forgiveness model for mediation work in organisations, useful for consultants, human resource specialists and counsellors in the field. Forgiveness, as Carroll discusses, tends to be seen in individual terms. Yet organisations carry considerable potential for causing damage both to employees and to the public. Carroll challenges the mindset that equates an organisation with a machine, an entity. He suggests that organisations can be seen as living organisms more like 'communities of people that have a life and being other than their being solely a collection of individuals'. If we can accept that, then we can consider the possibility that organisations can forgive and be forgiven.

Chapter 6 continues the theme of mediation, this time within the criminal justice system. Guy Masters explores the damaging impact both the crime and the traditional criminal justice system can have on the victim. Here the crime becomes a violation by the state, rather than a personal violation, potentially further disempowering the individual. He charts the development of the restorative justice movement, which seeks to give more justice to the victim and to offer both victim and perpetrator the opportunity to meet. Masters discusses shame based on the literature in the restorative justice field. He explores the notion of conferences (meetings) as places of shaming – within a supportive atmosphere – and reintegration for the perpetrator. Shaming, in these terms, is seen as positive – a stark contrast to the notion of shame in much of the psychotherapy literature.

Chapter 7 continues the discussion of restorative justice, here focusing on political trauma. Fathima Moosa, Gill Straker and Gill Eagle draw on decades of experience as psychotherapists working in South Africa with victims of apartheid-induced trauma. After offering an understanding of the work of the TRC, they alert the reader to the complexities of any decision to forgive for a person involved in political struggles. The decision will have intra-psychic, interpersonal and community implications. They carefully unpack the elements involved in making the decision whether or not to forgive, highlighting that for many, forgiveness involved a further sacrifice. The authors also offer a personal exploration of guilt and self-forgiveness as black and white therapists working with victims of political oppression.

In Chapter 8, Joy Green writes as a client about her journey towards healing and forgiveness with the aid of therapy. She had worked for many years in a helping profession, recognising the problems of others but not of herself. She talks of her guilt, given her strong Christian beliefs, at her need to seek therapy – feeling that her faith 'ought' to have been sufficient. As problems unfolded, she describes her struggle to stay with the process and it is clear that her choice of a Christian therapist with a similar value base was crucial to her. As therapists, we can theorise about the healing process, about how therapy can help someone move towards forgiveness. Joy Green offers the reader both the difficulties and the rewards of persevering with the process.

In the final chapter, Ransley and Spy contrast the thinking expressed in the chapters in this book with some of the American literature. They end by offering a framework for those working with individuals who have been traumatised by a wrong. This can lead to forgiveness, a moral decision not to forgive, self-forgiveness or some other road to healing. What's important is that individuals, hopefully, find a way of sufficiently coming to terms with what has happened so that they are no longer consumed by it and can begin to find their own, unique, path to moving on.

References

Arnold, A. (1998) *The Lost Art of Forgiving*. Robertsbridge, East Sussex: The Plough Publishing House.

Kosmin, B., Mayer, E. and Kayser, A. (2001) *American Religious Affiliation Survey*. New York: The Graduate Center, City University of New York.

Chapter 1

Forgiveness: themes and issues

Cynthia Ransley

'Teach me to forgive,' asks the disciple of his master in an ancient Indian story. 'If you had not condemned,' comes the reply, 'you would not have needed to forgive.'

(Soares-Prabhu 1986: 63)

In discussing forgiveness, do we not also have to grapple with the desire for revenge? When we have been wronged, how can we find some relief for our feelings of anger and distress? The ancient Greeks talked of the Furies who would pursue and torture wrong-doers and many of us may have longed, on occasions, for the support of the Furies. But we may also be influenced by our version of the Bible where God alone is allowed revenge: 'vengeance [is] mine; I will repay, saith the Lord' (Romans 12:19).

Murphy (1988) writes of 'retributive emotions': specific passions of anger, resentment and hatred which need to be diffused, not least for the sake of public order, into a criminal justice system. 'The criminal law gives distinct satisfaction for the desire for vengeance' wrote Stephen (1973). Justice is seen as retributive, offering the victim some direction for his or her anger. But many feel some discomfort at the thought of a purely retributional system of justice, even if restricted to 'an eye for an eye'. Various moral and religious traditions have come together with the view, in our culture, that we should transcend these feelings and that our desire for retribution be tempered by 'softer' emotions such as compassion, forgiveness and mercy. Justice is then, the argument goes, more likely to become restorative, seeking to rehabilitate the wrongdoer and ideally support the victim too. Restorative justice in the criminal justice system and in South Africa's Truth and

Reconciliation Commission (TRC) will be discussed in Chapters 6 and 7. In the Jewish tradition, even God acknowledges finding a balance is difficult. Murphy (1988: 14) quotes the Mahzhor for Yom Kippur: 'Even God prays. What is His prayer? May it be My will that My love of compassion overwhelm My demand for strict justice'. The criminal justice system and the biblical God reflect an individual's struggle between vengeful feelings or 'strict justice' and compassion or mercy. Individuals and societies differ on the balance they hold between the two.

This dichotomy needs to be borne in mind in this overview of some of the issues and current thinking on forgiveness. I look at various religious traditions as they provide much of the ethical basis for forgiveness and then explore the complexity of the term. I identify some American models of forgiveness and, finally, consider how we develop the capacity to forgive.

Religion and forgiveness

Many associate forgiveness with Christianity. But the notion of asking for and granting forgiveness is addressed in most main-stream religious traditions. Even where the discussion is limited, all focus on compassion and mercy. There are certain broad areas of difference between groups (and differences within traditions too). The first centres on repentance. Can you forgive someone who has not repented? Even if you want to, have you the right? The second area of difference is what is the purpose of forgiveness?

Hinduism

The notion of the mighty bestowing forgiveness, *ksama* or *ksamata*, on repentant human beings can be traced right back to the Vedic period (5000–1000 BCE) in India – long before the Bible. An example from the *Rig-Veda* is, 'Forgive me all the mistakes I have committed . . . O Lord of Love' (Easwaran 1991: 40). Beck writes that the mighty Lord Varuna was gracious to those who repented and would remove sins across several generations (Rye *et al.* 2000). Some Hindu stories describe divine forgiveness without repentance; in others it is a prerequisite.

Across the different traditions within Hinduism, concepts such as forgiveness, duty, compassion and forbearance are discussed in the epics and *dharma sastras*: they are seen as essential qualities for those who wish to follow the *dharma*, the path of righteousness. While Narayanan notes that nontheistic Hindu traditions, 'by definition, do not focus on divine forgiveness . . . in the Sri Vaishnava tradition . . . the Goddess Lakshmi/Sri is said to epitomise the quality of forgiveness and grace' (Rye *et al.* 2000: 29).

Buddhism

Given the variety of languages and traditions within Buddhism, there are difficulties in finding any exact equivalent of the word 'forgiveness'. The Buddhist notion of forbearance involves both enduring a wrong and renouncing anger towards someone who has offended you. The change of attitude required is highly valued (Rye *et al.* 2000).

Forbearance, compassion and pity are linked by Hallisey to the Buddha's First Noble Truth that 'all this [life] is suffering' (Rye *et al.* 2000: 27) and to Buddhists' dedication to ending suffering. Through compassion and pity, it is possible to empathise with the suffering of the offender and to take steps to relieve it. This is not linked to the wrongdoer repenting or expressing remorse. If the offender feels shame at the difference between his or her behaviour and the compassion of the wronged person, this may lead to a change of attitude. But what is crucial is compassion. Soares-Prabhu (1986: 57) tells the Buddhist story from the *Mahvagga* – reminiscent of the words of Martin Luther King or Gandhi – of the Prince of Kosola, who on remembering the advice of his dying father, spared the life of the man who had murdered his family and usurped his kingdom: 'Do not look far [i.e. do not let your hatred last long], do not look near [i.e. do not be quick to fall out with your friends], for hatred is not appeased by hatred, hatred is appeased by non-hatred alone'.

Judaism

Wittenberg (2001) would disagree. He argues that history has shown that 'justice cannot leave the protection of the oppressed to the gentle powers of mercy alone'. In the Jewish tradition, a wrongdoer must first repent and atone before being granted forgiveness. In the daily prayers and particularly in the ten days of repentance, culminating in Yom Kippur, the Day of Atonement, Jews confess their sins: 'For all these things, God of Forgiveness, forgive us, pardon us and grant us atonement' (from the confessional prayers of Yom Kippur, Wittenberg 2001: 63). Wittenberg notes the three parts to the prayer: 'Forgive us', a biblical term, involves turning to God in the first stage of atonement; 'pardon us', a rabbinical term, describes a human interaction – a request that the victim grants remission of the debt – thus, the wrongdoer is expected to ask forgiveness both of God and the victim; 'atonement' requires the wrongdoer to learn from mistakes in order not to repeat them and to make amends. Through this process both of repentance and returning to the right path, the wrongdoer is allowed to return – *teshuvah* – to the covenanted community.

Maimonides set out in detail The Laws of Forgiveness in the *Mishneh Torah*, around 1180. This includes asking the victim's forgiveness, in front of others, on up to three occasions. It is interesting how this avoids any notion that a quick, half-hearted apology will suffice. Once the wrongdoer has repented and been through the process of atonement, it becomes the *duty* of the victim to forgive (Dorff 1998). The duty is based both on imitating God's attitude to forgiveness and because the Law demands it. In forgiving, it is not essential that there will be reconciliation between victim and wrongdoer, but it opens the possibility. On the other hand, a person may decide to reconcile, have some relationship with the other, either where the wrongdoer does not repent or where the wrong was committed against another (e.g. the murder of a relative). In neither situation would forgiveness be appropriate.

The Jewish tradition does not look favourably on 'free' forgiveness. Unlike Buddhist values, it would see forgiving a wrongdoer who has not repented and been through the process of 'return' as potentially contrary to justice – undermining the social and religious pressures on the individual and thus increasing the possibility that the wrong will be repeated. Contrition is the necessary first step towards forgiveness.

Christianity

The readiness to forgive and be forgiven is central to Christianity. Indeed, as Soares-Prabhu (1986) writes, there is no community, no 'bread of life' unless there is also forgiveness. God's love and forgiveness is the central offering to Christians. Forgiveness is, then, a responsibility – and a way of being open to God's love.

This is epitomised in the Lord's Prayer: 'Forgive us our trespasses as we forgive those who trespass against us'. Jesus continues with the instruction: 'Yes, if you forgive others their failings, your heavenly father will forgive you yours; but if you do not forgive others, your father will not forgive your failings either' (Matthew 6:12, 14–15).

In the miracle of the paralysed man (Mark 2, 1–13), Jesus surprises those present by saying to him, 'My son, your sins are forgiven'. Some of the scribes were concerned by this and said, 'Who can forgive sins but God alone?' Jesus heals the man saying it is no more difficult for the Son of Man to forgive than to heal. Jesus shows he is the Son of God and extends the right of human beings to forgive.

Jewish Law demanded the punishment of the woman taken in adultery (John 8:7). Jesus utters the well-known words, 'Let he who is without sin among you be the first to throw a stone at her'. Jesus thus confronts the accusers and, as the one sinless person, forbears from throwing a stone. He goes a step beyond the law in showing mercy and the nature of undeserved love.

Unlike Judaism, Christian forgiveness does not depend on the repentance of the wrongdoer. This was epitomised by the last words of Christ on the cross, 'Father forgive them, they know not what they do' (Luke 23:34). Genuine forgiveness can lead the sinner to understand their wrongdoing and repent. Repentance is seen not so much as a precursor of forgiveness, as in the Jewish tradition, but as a crucial step in the direction of becoming a member of the Kingdom of God (McCullough and Worthington 1999).

Islam

Like Buddhism and Christianity, the Muslim is encouraged by the Qur'an to forgive irrespective of whether the person repents. Ali writes that the Qur'an taught a middle way between turning the other cheek and a blood feud: 'revenge to the extent harm done is allowed but forgiveness is preferred' (reminiscent of the earlier 'eye for an eye') both because Allah values forgiveness and it helps repair relationships (Rye *et al.* 2000: 31). Those who forgive instead of retaliating can expect a special blessing from God. Mohammad, like Jesus, offered a model of forgiveness in his lifetime to his followers by forgiving those who persecuted him.

The God, Allah, is the ultimate power who can forgive. One of his 99 attributes is Al-Ghafoor, the Forgiving One. Ali (Rye *et al.* 2000: 21) writes that forgiveness means 'closing an account or offense against God or any of His creation'. An offence against a human being is an offence against God and can be forgiven by God.

Forgiveness is offered to the extent that individuals desire to be forgiven themselves. Some scholars interpret the Qur'an as indicating that the search for forgiveness is 'more virtuous and nearer to God' than the search for justice (Hathout in McCullough and Worthington 1999).

In summary

I am indebted to the religious scholars whose work I have referenced, all of whom provide useful additional insights for those interested. Readers may find the comparisons offered by Rye *et al.* (2000) particularly useful. What is clear is that concepts akin to forgiveness are important in all the religious traditions discussed above, though some may wonder at the difference between the early teachings on forgiveness and the vengeful behaviour practised by some factions, in the name of religion, up to the present day.

The Jewish tradition differs sharply from the others. Transgressors must repent – seek *teshuvah* – before being offered forgiveness. The others place value on offering forgiveness (or, for the Buddhists, acting with forbearance and compassion) irrespective of the repentance of the wrongdoer. There are various rationales for forgiving: to imitate God, religious duty, to seek God's forgiveness, the path of righteousness, to repair relationships. Only Buddhism does not have a word for forgiveness, though elements of it appear to be encompassed in Buddhist culture. Yet what precisely does forgiveness mean? Can we be confident that there is a shared meaning across cultural and language differences?

What is forgiveness?

When people speak or write of forgiveness, they mean different things. The differences reflect their value base and perhaps their motivation for forgiving. For Watson (1984: 149) who comes from a Christian perspective, forgiveness is about love. He quotes McCall's words, 'Fore-give-ness is love given *before* another has either given it, earned it, accepted it, or even understood it. That is the nature of God's love who sent his Son to bear this long before we ever thought of loving him. Love takes the initiative'. Watson continues that when we have been badly hurt, we may not have the capacity to love the person who has wronged us, but we can get strength from God's love which 'can be continuously poured into our hearts by the Holy Spirit'.

In the political arena, Gandhi's view of forgiveness was specifically about non-violence: 'Abstinence [from retaliation] is forgiveness . . .' He goes on to underline that for forgiveness to be authentic it must come from a person who has found his or her strength and 'when there is the power to punish; it is meaningless when it pretends to proceed from a helpless creature. A mouse hardly forgives a cat when it allows itself to be swallowed by her'. Reassuringly, he sees it not as submission but as putting 'one's whole soul against the will of the tyrant' (in Soares-Prabhu 1986: 65).

These are two very different definitions: forgiveness as undeserved love and forgiveness as non-violent retaliation, one focusing on emotion and the other on behaviour. The psychology and psychotherapy literature offers a range of definitions for forgiveness. These include:

- releasing resentment towards an offender (Hargrave 1994);
- restoring relationships and healing inner emotional wounds (DiBlasio and Proctor 1993).

In these terms, forgiveness is a psychological construct as well as a social one, involving changes within the person as well as being in relation to someone else. When we are thinking of forgiveness, it is important to be aware of both elements, though the change may only take place in one – and some writers focus more on one element than the other.

The same word is used across the whole range of transgressions from minor to those of a particularly vicious nature. Is a particular attitude required of the victim for there to be forgiveness? I find Enright and the Human Development Study Group's definition offers useful clarification (and I will refer back to it at various points in the chapter): 'a willingness to abandon one's right to resentment, negative judgment and indifferent behavior toward one who unjustly hurt us, while fostering the undeserved qualities of compassion, generosity and even love toward him or her' (Enright *et al.* 1998: 46–7).

Imagine being attacked, physically or verbally. You may well feel shock, distress or shame. Rather than simply internalising the hurt, it is healthy to feel anger towards the person who attacked. This emanates from having a sufficient sense of self and self-worth. The question of how to 'abandon one's right to resentment' and 'negative judgment' towards the offender is a complex one. Does it necessarily involve forgiveness? We may just forget about it. We are in a meeting and someone criticises us. If the criticism was mild, the person is usually kind and we are feeling confident, we may only half notice it. We get involved in the discussion and the words slip from our memory (though it is interesting how they may reappear if the person behaves in the same way again). Some people are less quick to take offence and this can be useful in social relationships, though therapists may wonder if they are using some unconscious strategy such as denial or dissociation as a protection. Given that forgetting is largely involuntary, surely this cannot be equated with forgiveness.

Can we talk about forgiveness after an accident? We stop at traffic lights and the car behind smashes into us. As we start shouting at the driver, he says there's no point getting angry with him, the brakes failed. We start weighing up whether it was purely an 'accident'. Was he careless about servicing his car? Then he says it's a hired car so he's not responsible. Or we may feel angry when our toddler drops our favourite vase on the floor and it smashes. Yet we know the infant does not understand either the importance of the vase or his or her ability to hold it safely. The right to resentment and negative judgement – and therefore forgiveness – is surely only relevant where the person is capable of carrying responsibility for the wrong, a 'responsible wrongdoer' as Hampton (1988) puts it.

If we accept Enright's definition that forgiveness involves abandoning negative judgement towards a wrongdoer, how do we do that without condoning unacceptable behaviour? When I was a hospital social worker, I saw one woman, several times, in casualty after being beaten up by her partner. 'It's all right,' she would say, 'he was drunk.' One time she said she forgave him, but was it forgiveness? I believe she was condoning his behaviour. As Hampton (1988) so interestingly discusses, condoning involves some self-deception in which you accept, without protest, either inward or outward, unacceptable behaviour towards yourself. (And perhaps fear pushes you to pretend to yourself it's OK.) If the behaviour is not wrong – or the person isn't capable of carrying responsibility for it – then they aren't guilty and there is no reason to have feelings about it. This has echoes of colluding: acting as a bystander (Clarkson 1996), pretending wrongful behaviour towards another is not happening. At some level, condoning is not compatible with self-respect and collusion with respect of self and/or other.

There is a real paradox in forgiveness. If forgiveness does involve a change of heart, abandoning resentment and negative judgement, can you really do this without, at least to some extent, condoning the person's behaviour? Hampton (1988) comes to the conclusion that the defining quality of forgiveness is that it involves a person revising his or her judgement of the wrongdoer and reaching an honest decision that the person is still morally decent *despite* the behaviour. But, in no way, she says, does it involve giving up opposition to the wrongdoer's action or character trait.

This clarification is useful for two reasons. First it gets round the seeming inconsistency that it is possible to forgive and yet still pursue legal redress or some other type of compensation. Second, it offers the *potential* for accepting and reconciling with the individual while being clear that the action was unacceptable. Reconciliation, a two-way process in which there is a return to being in relationship, is seen as separate from forgiveness in the literature. Individuals may decide that they can forgive the other in terms of seeing them as basically morally decent, but (as an example) they don't trust them not to be violent in the future and so are unwilling to reconcile.

But are we all basically morally decent?

If forgiveness involves seeing people as basically morally decent despite their behaviour, can we say that *all* individuals are morally decent or do some lose their right to this by their actions? Casaarjian appears able to value the intrinsic goodness of all humans. He speaks of going beyond the limits of another's personality and actions, 'to see a pure essence, unconditioned by personal history, that has limitless potential and is always worthy of respect or love' (1992: 23).

However, as far back as the twelfth century, Maimonides gave a list of crimes, so heinous that the perpetuator could not be forgiven, even by God (Dorff 1998). Yet, he was not absolute in his condemnation. He said that if the offender repented and died while going through the process of return into the covenanted community, he or she 'will have a portion in the world to come' (Dorff 1998: 51). The defining feature was the person's willingness to abandon the wrongful behaviour, meaningfully confess and atone. Does that make the person morally decent again, no matter how appalling the offence? If you have wronged someone, though not in an 'appalling' fashion, and you continue to deny it, can you be called 'morally decent'?

This inevitably raises the complex question of evil. Socrates argued that we should pity the wrongdoer as no one is intentionally wicked and virtue is a matter of knowledge. The French philosopher Comte-Sponville (2003: 123) argues against this position. Evil, he writes, is not an error: 'Evil is a matter of will, not ignorance; a matter of heart not intelligence or mind; a matter of hatred not stupidity . . . evil is selfishness, wickedness, cruelty'. In fact it is only such acts, done *on purpose*, his argument goes, which require our forgiveness. He quotes Jankélévitch's words: 'We excuse the ignorant, we forgive the wicked'.

North (1998) writes that such cases pose the ultimate challenge to forgiveness because of the nature of the moral and psychological questions. Crimes such as child torture or genocide, she suggests, are so horrific or on such a scale that they can defy our understanding. Attempts at setting the wrong in context may reinforce our perspective that the perpetrator is morally bad. And in a few cases, the wrongdoer may actually appear to take sadistic pleasure in harming others.

The question of choice is central to the debate. Does the person know what he or she is doing? As the popular press would put it, is the individual 'mad or bad?' A sadist or incapacitated by psychosis or a severe personality disorder? Holmgren (in North 1998: 28) argues that an individual who has in Kantian terms 'lost the capacity for goodwill' cannot be held morally responsible for their actions and the appropriate attitude is compassion.

The social psychologist, Baumeister (1999), researched the ways people justify violence and cruelty from small transgressions to murder or torture. He believes that 'pure evil', sadistic pleasure at brutality, is largely a myth. Evil behaviour is learned and comes out of ordinary human attributes like ambition, fear, pride or idealism. Evil actions occur gradually as self-control breaks down because of group pressure or small decisions. He concludes that most perpetrators do not see what they are doing as wicked. They see themselves as victims correcting a wrong. He gives the example of Nazis who set out to correct the (real) injustices of the post World War I Versailles treaty.

His interesting book may go some way to helping us – sometimes – to understand actions which, as North (1988) puts it, defy understanding. Whether we can then feel compassion or able to forgive the perpetrator will link to an extent to the level of harm the wrong has done us. But our response will also reflect our personality, our culture and personal values. It will be influenced by the way we have been treated and judged. It may also link with the rationale we have for forgiving. The next section will look at some of the reasons the therapeutic literature offers for forgiving.

Why forgive?

In the psychology and psychotherapy literature, there are a number of reasons given for forgiving. While some have ethical undertones, compared with religious texts there is a shift of emphasis towards self-interest.

Forgiveness as a 'gift for the self'?

Some of the current forgiveness research explores what the benefits of developing the capacity to forgive have on the psychological well-being of the individual. Enright et al. (1998) report some positive findings on work with incest survivors, 'parentally love-deprived' students and elderly women (see also Worthington 1998; Enright and Fitzgibbons 2000). Baures (1996: 89) is quite clear: 'Forgiveness is not meant for the abuser but for the survivor who realises that hate is self destructive'. She points to the damage resentment and bitterness does to the individual, to his or her relationships with the wrongdoer and other people.

The self-help literature emphasises this. Rowe (1996) writes that the advantage of forgiveness is that we are freed from being the object of another's actions. It involves the person making the decision not to be dominated by his or her feelings about another's behaviour and, in forgiving, takes back control of their life. This, Rowe says, brings with it an increase in self-esteem.

Is the term 'forgiveness' appropriate when it is purely a 'gift for the self'? Ralph is overwhelmed by resentment and bitterness towards his neighbour. He is so agitated that he decides to have some hypnosis. It works, Ralph becomes less stressed and, in the process, the negative feelings and judgements drop away. Is this forgiving, or merely some version of forgetting? Must there be some element of *morality*, of an offering to the other person, if we are to call it forgiveness?

Many would agree with Murphy (1988: 24) that 'forgiveness is not the overcoming of resentment *simpliciter*; it is rather this: forswearing resentment on moral grounds'. Enright and North (1998:19) write that the essence of forgiveness is 'outward-looking and other-directed' – it is principally an action towards another. In these terms, the lessening of resentment and an increase of self-esteem are useful by-products of forgiveness rather than the only goal.

Forgiveness as a 'gift' to the other person – a way of developing relationships?

For Melanie Klein, our own needs and our ability to love others are inextricably linked. She wrote of the value for the child of being able to forgive his or her parents. If, deep in our unconscious minds, we have been able to rid ourselves, to some extent, of grievances towards our parents (or caretakers), 'and have forgiven them for the frustrations we had to bear, then we can be at peace with ourselves and are able to love others in the true sense of the word' (1988: 343).

North (1998) suggests that forgiveness is a demonstration of our ability, as human beings, to be both rational and spiritual, capable of offering 'moral love' to someone who does not merit it. This influenced Enright's definition (see p. 16) that forgiveness involves developing *undeserved compassion* towards the other person. The challenge is to be able to offer this from a place of respect for the other person and confident of our own strength and not – using Gandhi's analogy – from the 'mouse' in us.

Perhaps there is always more than one motivation for forgiveness. People who belong to a religious or political group which holds forgiveness central to their value system may be motivated to forgive to be true to their cultural or faith beliefs, maintain their standing in the community and as a way of improving relationships. Moosa, Eagle and Straker (Chapter 7) offer a valuable insight into the complexity of motivation in South Africa's TRC where there was a clear attempt to avoid spiralling negative cycles of resentment and vengeful actions. As Archbishop Tutu said, 'forgiveness is realpolitik in the long run' (Greer 1998).

Forgiveness as a misuse of power?

Let me end this section with a note of caution about the potential misuses of forgiveness. If we agree that forgiveness is more than letting go of resentment and that it involves offering a 'gift' to another who does not deserve it, then we must not underestimate the difficulty of doing this from a place of respect. In the research I discuss in Chapter 3, a number of people remembered times when they had resented being forgiven for behaviour they saw as perfectly acceptable. If we are forgiven by people who believe they hold the moral truth and are willing to accept us 'sin and all' surely there is the danger they are coming from a place of superiority, hoping we, the 'wrongdoer', will come round to seeing the error of our ways? Enright *et al.* (1998) use the expression 'pseudo forgiveness' to describe the situation where forgiveness is being used to maintain or gain power. They also use it to describe the action of a person who feels coerced to forgive from fear or duty.

The motivation for forgiveness, therefore, may be self-interest, social, moral, stem from a strong sense of identification with a group – or a combination of these. The question, surely, is how can we achieve it? But first, we must look at how people react when they are wronged.

The response to being wronged

Worthington (1998) equates our physiological response to being hurt or rejected with classic fear conditioning in which we first freeze as we tense in the face of danger and then move into a fight-flight stress response, submitting if neither is possible. He offers a detailed argument that 'unforgiveness' is based on fear conditioning, though he admits that some researchers argue that it is anger-based.

Hargrave and Sells (1997) point to four basic responses in people who feel their trust and love has been violated. Some experience rage and uncontrollable anger towards the wrongdoer while others tend towards shame, accusing themselves of being unworthy of love. In future relationships, some tend towards being over-controlled as they try to minimise hurt while others act chaotically, assuming they can do little to prevent being hurt again. It may be useful to think of these responses in terms of a continuum between anger and shame and another between over-control and chaos. Some people will tend to be at one end of the continuum, while others will oscillate in their response – at certain times shame may be figural and anger more in the background. At another time, the position may reverse.

The issue of power is crucial in an insult. People speak of feeling used, degraded, demeaned by the other. Lampen (1994) writes that the injury can feel such a personal attack that the individual may lose the sense of human solidarity, provoking fear of disintegration. Neimeyer and Anderson (2002) write of the challenge to reconstruct meaning after a loss. Some offences may be experienced as beyond comprehension or unforgivable if they challenge what Janoff-Bulman and Berg (Neimeyer and Anderson 2002: 48) describe as our 'assumptive world' – our unspoken beliefs that, for example, the world is benevolent, that there is justice or God will protect us from harm. Recovery can be arduous as the person negotiates making sense of what seems senseless, finding some benefit or constructing some new theory about life and living as well as developing a new sense of personal identity and roles.

Towards forgiveness

A number of models have been developed in the USA to describe the process of forgiveness. I will look at three of them. In Chapter 5, Carroll gives details of a further model developed by Smedes. There are, generally, certain similarities. First, forgiveness is seen as involving an active decision, though there are variations in how early in the process a person makes that decision. While empathy is seen as pivotal, it is rarely mentioned as a need the victim will have. Almost all the models include:

- developing empathy for the wrongdoer;
- regaining a more balanced view;

- letting go of resentment;
- giving up the right to punish.

Forgiveness, in these terms, appears to be a complex process involving both a change in motivation, affect and cognition, possibly resulting in changes in behaviour.

Four stations of forgiveness

Hargrave (in Hargrave and Sells 1997) offers a model of forgiveness from a family therapy perspective. The use of the word '*stations*' in forgiveness avoids the sense of a linear stage approach: people oscillate between stations many times as they seek to restore trust in the relationship and forgive. If the wrongdoer is not willing, or able, to be involved in the process, as is often the case, the first two stations apply. The final two stations involve both parties.

- **Exonerating**. Hargrave describes this as the 'effort of lifting the load of culpability off the person who caused the hurt' (in Hargrave and Sells 1997: 44). It is achieved through:

  Station 1: developing insight into how the wrong has happened, including awareness of family patterns. This leads to

  Station 2: developing understanding or identification with the wrongdoer.

- **Forgiving**. For Hargrave, this involves a response by the person who caused the injustice (this links with earlier discussions in this chapter on whether forgiveness depends on repentance). The final two stations are:

  Station 3: giving the opportunity for compensation. The person wronged gives the wrongdoer the chance to take responsibility and act in ways which will progressively help trust develop.

  Station 4: the overt act of forgiving. The two people discuss what has happened and agree they will seek a trustworthy relationship in the future.

Hargrave's 'forgiving' is similar to what some writers (e.g. Worthington 1998) call reconciliation.

Promoting forgiveness

In other models (e.g. Donnelly in Baures 1996; Enright *et al.* 1998; Smedes 1998; Worthington 1998), forgiveness does not necessarily involve any action by the wrongdoer. Over the last ten years a number of programmes have focused on *teaching forgiveness* as a psychological health intervention. Enright's model, which involves 20 units, is used in many of the programmes (see e.g. www.forgivenessday.org and Enright *et al.* 1998). Masters offers further detail of the model in Chapter 6.

The process model of forgiveness

Uncovering phase. This involves:

- the person becoming aware that they were wronged after examining the defences used, such as denial, to defend against the hurt;
- confronting the impact the wrongdoing has had on an emotional level – this may well include anger, shame, distress – the time spent dwelling on what happened, comparing him or herself with the wrongdoer, the negative impact on his or her life and view of the world.

Decision phase. Here the person is aware that his or her response is not working, considers forgiveness as an alternative and then whether to make the commitment.

Work phase. The commitment is supported by the person being encouraged to take a wider view of the wrongdoer, not in terms of excusing but by becoming aware of their vulnerabilities. This 'enlarged' view may lead to empathy and compassion. In turn, the individual makes a commitment '*not* to pass on the pain of the injury to others, including the offender' (Enright *et al.* 1998: 54). Forgiveness is, therefore, a decision based on a moral willingness to absorb the pain. This exemplifies the 'gift-life quality of forgiveness'.

Deepening phase. The person begins to find meaning and perhaps a new purpose as a result of his or her suffering and the forgiveness process. They feel some release and feel less alone.

Readers may find the acronym **REACH**, which Worthington (1998) uses, a useful reminder of the similar stages in his model:

- **R**ecall the hurt
- **E**mpathise with the one who hurt you
- **A**ltruistic gift of forgiveness (make an)
- **C**ommitment to forgive
- **H**old onto the forgiveness.

   In some of the literature, the therapist is acting as an educator 'teaching' forgiveness to groups or is actively working with the client towards the goal of forgiveness. Many therapists will balk at being so directive: it will go against their philosophy or style of practice. However, any summary inevitably devalues the extent of the thinking involved in the development of the ideas and for this, the reader must go to the primary texts. It is evident for Worthington that developing empathy for the wrongdoer leads to the decision to forgive, whereas for Enright the decision comes first. To an extent this relates to whether forgiveness is seen as a by-product of a change of emotional attitude and thinking.

   Discussion of forgiveness in the psychoanalytic literature is less prominent, Durham (2000) being a notable exception. Galdston, who comes from an object relations perspective, is clear that forgiveness is not the replacement of negative, hateful feelings with loving ones: 'Forgiveness is accomplished by recovering the aggression which has been pre-empted by the desire for revenge and redirecting it towards a new goal . . . With forgiveness, the blocking introject loses its significance. The goal of revenge passes' (Durham 2000: 78). The sense of the introject losing its significance is a far cry from the cognitive and moral decision to forgive. Durham takes this further. To Durham, forgiveness, or the relinquishing of vengeance, involves the loss of a self-object, 'the energizing, satisfying pursuit of "sweet" revenge' (p. 108) and, therefore, involves the process of mourning.

   Coping with loss or injustice often brings a loss of confidence or a drop in self-esteem. As a precursor to any change of heart, whether transcending resentment, mourning or giving up the pursuit of revenge, individuals must *regain* (or develop) sufficient confidence in themselves. There is much talk of offering empathy. What is given too little attention in the literature is the victim's *need* for empathy. An empathic therapeutic relationship in which the person can face any sense of shame about being deceived or about putting up with wrongful behaviour – i.e. offer self-forgiveness – and can share the distress and anger at the other's actions, is, in my view, of fundamental importance in the process.

Before ending this section, it is important to acknowledge that there is a body of opinion that people can achieve emotional release and find some peace with the past without forgiveness. This will be addressed in Chapter 3. The remainder of this chapter will tentatively address the question of when and how people develop the capacity to forgive.

Developing a forgiving personality

Enright *et al.* (1989) researched a developmental model of forgiveness in the USA, versions of which were tested in Taiwan and Korea. These studies suggest that age has an effect on how we conceptualise both justice and forgiveness and that our willingness to forgive develops through our life span. The results showed no gender variation, nor differences between Asia and the USA. In the studies, participants were given scenarios with dilemmas and asked to choose how they might respond: the responses offered corresponded to six stages of forgiveness (see Mullet and Girard 2000 for more detail):

- **Revengeful forgiveness**: I can forgive when I punish so they suffer as much pain as I did.
- **Conditional or restitutional forgiveness**: I can forgive if I get back what they took from me. The mean score observed in children around 9 or 10 was near this point.
- **Expectational forgiveness**: I can forgive if people close to me think it's what I should do even if what was taken hasn't been restored. The mean score for 15–16-year-olds was around here.
- **Lawful expectational forgiveness**: I forgive because of the expectations of my philosophy/religion. This was the mean score for young and middle-aged adults.
- **Forgiveness as social harmony**: I forgive in order to restore good relationships.

- **Forgiveness as love**: I forgive because I really care for each individual and want to keep open the possibility of reconciliation.

Despite the theories on forgiveness discussed in previous sections, few in the samples identified with the final category. Mullet and Girard (2000) refer to their own research which showed that elderly people were more willing to forgive than younger adults. Maybe our perspective softens as we realise we have made mistakes, that we have survived the mistakes and wrongs of others?

I wonder to what extent the participants' responses to theoretical dilemmas reflects how forgiving they are in their daily lives: I am mindful of McCullough and Worthington's (1999) research in which religious people were rated higher on the disposition to forgive in general terms, but the difference was not strong when it came to real-life circumstances. Mullet and Girard (2000) also urge some caution as the responses clearly depend on the relevance and variety of the scenarios and this may have impacted, particularly, on the younger children's responses. These provisos apart, there seems reasonable evidence that the propensity to forgive has a developmental character which extends over the entire life span.

When does forgiveness start?

If you look back to the six levels of forgiveness above, the first two are about revenge and restitution. Only the final four are about forgiveness, which Enright *et al.* (1998) linked to adolescence. While being mindful of Mullet and Girard's (2000) reservations, these findings are interesting as they reflect the views of some other theorists.

Piaget (1932) contrasted forgiveness with justice, the main focus of his book. He suggested that forgiveness is more than 'mathematical reciprocity'; it involves a sense of 'ideal reciprocity': you forgive because you have been forgiven in the past and so that you will be forgiven in the future. Given the complexity of the reasoning, he placed the ability to forgive in late childhood.

I referred earlier to Durham's view that, as part of the healing process, forgiveness can be looked upon as 'an intrinsic, positive part of *mourning the passage of revenge*' (2000: 70). Freud saw mourning as 'detaching the libido, bit by bit' and for Durham this characterises the painstakingly slow process of forgiveness. She refers to Wolfenstein's view that a child is not capable of the gradual decathexis necessary for mourning until adolescence (Durham 2000: 107). However, in Durham's work with young children, she has seen their ability to gradually let go of feelings of vengeance, through repetitive play, as early as 5 years of age. The child then develops a more favourable view of the object of his or her fury and can redirect energy into other activities.

Whether this is forgiveness depends on your definition of the term. Durham thinks, in order to forgive, a child needs to have some understanding of rights and realise that he or she has been wronged. There is a vast difference between a young child's and an adult's understanding of this. There are also wide variations in personality. An anxious, diffident child may be slow to believe in his or her rights and think in terms of forgiving others rather than being forgiven. A narcissistic child, feeling entitled to have his or her needs met, may be slow to forgive. I commend the reader to Durham's interesting account of issues of revenge and forgiveness in relation to two very different character styles: the exploited-repressive patient and the vindictive character.

The child is probably not capable of understanding forgiveness and moving beyond, as Durham (2000: 13) puts it, 'the excitement, pleasures and pain of revenge, until he is capable of graduating from the "good guy/bad guy" stage of development'. The child needs to have developed enough faith in his or her own goodness to feel able to make reparations. Likewise the child needs to have developed the capacity to experience the other person, initially a parent or carer, as being a 'whole' person with both good and bad qualities. Cooper and Gilbert usefully develop these ideas in Chapter 4. Developing the capacity for concern as well for making reparations is crucial to the ability to offer forgiveness to self or other.

All this rests on the parent, or carer, having met the child's need for empathic attunement – at least to a reasonable degree. We need to have experienced empathy if we are to develop the capacity to empathise with others and with ourselves. This is essential for us to be able to gradually let go of the hurt another has caused or the shame and guilt at an error of our own.

Conclusion

Research is increasingly being developed on the role of forgiveness in psychological well-being and it seems likely that there will be a move into exploring possible links between forgiveness and physical health. Over the next ten years, the validity of the links should become clearer.

My aim in this chapter has been to offer the reader an overview of some of the issues and themes in the current literature on forgiveness including a discussion of its roots in various religious traditions. There are clearly different meanings given to the word 'forgiveness' and the motivation behind forgiveness is also complex. In general terms, forgiveness is based on the capacity to empathise with the wrongdoer and – gradually – let go of resentment. Our capacity to do this is inevitably influenced by our personality, culture (including faith and political beliefs) and above all by the way we have been treated and judged. What is little mentioned is our need – where we have been unjustly treated – to be offered empathy, to experience the empathy of others. This will be one of the themes explored in later chapters.

References

Baumeister, R. (1999) *Evil: Inside Human Violence and Cruelty*. New York: W.H. Freeman and Company.

Baures, M. (1996) Letting go of bitterness and hate, *Journal of Humanistic Psychology*, 36(1): 75–90.

Casaarjian, R. (1992) *Forgiveness, Bold Choice for a Peaceful Heart*. New York: Bantam Books.

Clarkson, P. (1996) *The Bystander*. London: Whurr.

Comte-Sponville, A. (2003) *A Short Treatise on the Great Virtues*. London: Vintage.

DiBlasio, F.A. and Proctor, J.H. (1993) Therapists and the clinical use of forgiveness, *American Journal of Family Therapy*, 21: 175–84.

Dorff, E.N. (1998) The elements of forgiveness: a Jewish approach, in E. Worthington (ed.) *Dimensions of Forgiveness*. Radnor, PA: Templeton Foundation Press.

Durham, M.S. (2000) *The Therapist's Encounters with Revenge and Forgiveness*. London: Jessica Kingsley.

Easwaran, E. (1991) *God Makes the Rivers Flow*. Tomales, CA: Nilgiri Press.

Enright, R. and Fitzgibbons, R. (2000) *Helping Clients Forgive: An Empirical Guide for Resolving Anger and Restoring Hope*. Washington: American Psychological Association.

Enright, R., Freedman, S. and Rique, J. (1998) The psychology of interpersonal forgiveness, in R.D. Enright and J. North (eds) *Exploring Forgiveness*. Madison, WI: University of Wisconsin Press.

Enright, R. and North, J. (eds) (1998) *Exploring Forgiveness*. Madison, WI: University of Wisconsin Press.

Enright, R.D., Santos, M.J.O. and Al-Mabuk, R.H. (1989) The adolescent as a forgiver, *Journal of Adolescence*, 12: 95–110.

Greer, C. (1998) The world is hungry for goodness, www.forgiveness-day.org/tutu.htm.

Hampton, J. (1988) Forgiveness, resentment and hatred, in J. Murphy and J. Hampton (eds), *Forgiveness and Mercy*. Cambridge, MA: Cambridge University Press.

Hargrave, T.D. (1994) *Families and Forgiveness*. New York: Brunner/Mazel.

Hargrave, T.D. and Sells, J.N. (1997) The development of a forgiveness scale, *Journal of Marital and Family Therapy*, 23(1): 41–62.

Klein, M. (1988) *Love, Guilt and Reparation and Other Works, 1921–1945*. London: Virago.

Lampen, J. (1994) *Mending Hurts*. London: Quaker Home Service.

McCullough, M.E. and Worthington, E.L. (1999) Religion and the forgiving personality, *Journal of Personality*, 67: 6.

McCullough, M.E., Pargament, K.I. and Thoresen, C.E. (2000) The psychology of forgiveness, in M.E. McCullough, K.I. Pargament and C.E. Thoresen (eds) *Forgiveness: Theory, Research and Practice*. New York: The Guilford Press.

Mullet, E. and Girard, M. (2000) Developmental and cognitive points of view of forgiveness, in M.E. McCullough, K.I. Pargament and C.E. Thoresen (eds) *Forgiveness: Theory, Research and Practice*. New York: The Guilford Press.

Murphy, J. (1988) The retributive emotions, in J. Murphy and J. Hampton (eds) *Forgiveness and Mercy*. Cambridge, MA: Cambridge University Press.

Neimeyer, R.A. and Anderson, A. (2002) Meaning reconstruction theory, in N. Thompson (ed.) *Loss and Grief*. Basingstoke: Palgrave.

North, J. (1998) The 'ideal' of forgiveness: a philosopher's exploration, in R.E. Enright and J. North (eds) *Exploring Forgiveness*. Madison, WI: University of Winsconsin Press.

Piaget, J. (1932) *The Moral Judgment of the Child*. London: Routledge & Kegan Paul.

Rowe, D. (1996) Depression and happiness, in S. Palmer, S. Dainow and P. Milner (eds) *Counselling*. London: Sage.

Rye, M.S., Pargament, K.I., Ali, M.A., Beck, G.L., Dorff, E.N., Hallisey, C., Narayan, V. and Williams, J.G. (2000) Religious perspectives on forgiveness, in M.E. McCullough, K.I. Pargament and C.E. Thoresen (eds) *Forgiveness: Theory, Research and Practice*. New York: The Guilford Press.

Smedes, L.B. (1984) *Forgive and Forget*. New York: Harper & Row.

Smedes, L.B. (1998) Stations on the journey from forgiveness to hope, in E.L. Worthington (ed.) *Dimensions of Forgiveness*. Radnor, PA: Templeton Foundation Press.

Soares-Prabhu, G. (1986) 'As we forgive': interhuman forgiveness in the teaching of Jesus, in C. Floristan and C. Duquoc (eds) *Concilium: Forgiveness*. Edinburgh: T&T Clark.

Stephen, J.F. (1973) *A History of the Criminal Law in England*. New York: Burt Franklin.

Watson, D. (1984) *Fear No Evil*. London: Hodder & Stoughton.

Wittenberg, J. (2001) Between memory and forgiveness, *The Jewish Quarterly*, Autumn: 63–6.

Worthington, E.L. (ed.) (1998) *Dimensions of Forgiveness*. Radnor, PA: Templeton Foundation Press. www.forgivenessday.org

Chapter 2

Christianity, therapy and forgiveness

Terri Spy

> Bear with each other and forgive whatever grievances you may have against one another. Forgive as the Lord forgave you.
>
> (Colossians 3:13)

Introduction

One of the most interesting issues I have noticed over my years as a therapist has been how much forgiveness, or difficulty with it, comes into my practice. I discovered, when I compared my experience with my peers, that this was unusual. Most people with whom I work do not have a committed Christian faith. They hold what I would see as Christian morals, beliefs and attitudes, such as kindness to people, not judging, being honest and treating others with respect. It is, generally, not their biblical faith that brings them to the theme of forgiveness, but their need to be at one with themselves and not feel judged by themselves or others.

In this chapter, I discuss my value base and the influences this has on my practice in general and, specifically, in relation to forgiveness. I then explore the work I do with Christian and non-Christian clients on the subject of forgiveness. Finally, I will offer a model that may be useful for therapists working in this field. In the case examples I give, names and details have been changed to preserve confidentiality. The biblical references I make in this chapter all come from the New International Version of the Bible.

My value base

I believe we are made in God's image and therefore we can become more in tune with God's concept for us. We can change our lives, if that is what we want, regardless of our faith or religious beliefs. I link this view with Rogers (1961) who believed that all forms of life, human beings included, have a tendency towards more complex organisation and fulfilling their potential. Rogers saw each individual as having a capacity for self-actualisation: the capacity for self-understanding, for self-directed behaviour and to change and develop. He believed that all that was needed for change to occur was a therapeutic relationship based on his core conditions of empathy, unconditional positive regard and congruence. Rogers was brought up in a Christian faith and spent two years in a theological college (Thorne 1992). What he was putting forward was, in many respects, similar to Christian beliefs.

I state my faith at the beginning of a therapeutic relationship, so that the client knows where I stand. I try to be open, honest and clear, and name the conditions of worth from which I work. I am equally open in asking, at an initial session, about the client's religious or faith beliefs. I have never found any discord caused by my raising the issue of faith or religion. The client can then decide whether or not he or she wants me as a therapist. Often our clients come having had little power over life choices. Therefore, I hold that it is of the utmost importance to demonstrate my true support for the client making positive choices, even if that means they choose not to work with me. A client's choice of therapist will depend on a number of variables, including gender, race and temperament. Religion, or faith, is one aspect of the choice.

With practising Christians, there is one further choice I offer during my contracting with them. I ask if they would like to pray at the start of each session. If this is important for them, we will pray together. If they do not wish to pray, this is also acceptable to me.

There have been a few occasions when I have chosen not to work with a person because of their religious beliefs. I would not work with someone who is active within the Jehovah's Witness religion or is a medium or spiritualist as our beliefs are so fundamentally different. I would also decline to work with a person who wants to explore making a life decision which would oppose my Christian values – for example, abortion. I have had clients – with whom I already had a working relationship – who became pregnant and wanted to discuss having an abortion. This I have been unable to do. I have shared with them the danger that I might try to influence them to my way of thinking on abortion, persuade them to do what I feel is right, rather than help them make their own choice. In these cases, I have encouraged them to seek other help for this decision.

Deep religious roots

> But that you may know that the Son of Man has authority on earth to forgive sins.
>
> (Mark 2:10)

There is much written in the Bible about forgiveness. Jesus, for example, repeatedly released people from the sins (offences) they had committed against others. In the parable of the paralysed man, Jesus says 'son, your sins are forgiven' (Mark 2:5). People, at the time, were outraged by his words as God alone has the power to forgive. Knowing what they were thinking, Jesus challenged them to consider what was easier, to say 'your sins are forgiven or take up your bed and walk' (Mark 2:9). The fact that he was God meant he could say both. Christianity is based on the belief that Jesus is the Son of God – and is God – has authority to forgive sins, heal the sick and has unlimited understanding of human beings.

McCullough and Worthington (1999) suggest there has been a tendency to overlook the deep religious roots of forgiveness. Forgiveness is spiritual, timeless and transcendent. The authors write that forgiveness begs questions about human fallibility and vulnerability.

As a therapist who is a practising Christian, the whole basis of my life is connected with my faith beliefs. For me, this has to be within a living faith and central to this is forgiveness. For the Christian, forgiveness brings release. I believe forgiveness enables us to live lives that can be filled with the ability to reconcile because forgiveness is a gift, an act of mercy. It is the path to healing. For true repentance and forgiveness, the person must come to terms with the past, in the light of what he or she knows now, in order to move on.

Within the psychotherapeutic community, therapists can take 'unconditional positive regard' (Rogers 1961) to mean that all aspects of the human condition are acceptable. I believe that, in an ideal world, this would be valid as good would prevail. However, although I hold that we are born with basic goodness, we are, thereafter, inevitably impacted by our relationships, particularly in childhood, and this may leave us with poor self-concept. Our beliefs and motivations become more complex and negative as a result of the care we received and the values and beliefs of our environment. I hold that unconditional positive regard, therefore, can only be possible in relation to the basic humanity of a person rather than his or her actions. Forgiveness is, therefore, in relation to the humanity of the person, rather than the action itself.

Forgiveness and the Bible

I am mindful of Leviticus (19:18): 'Love your neighbour as your self'. I believe in the fundamental interconnectedness of love and forgiveness. I cannot hold unforgivingness against another and still claim to love. So how can I love myself, if I am unable to forgive? How can I love another if I am unable to love myself?

This can only be done by acknowledging and letting go of negative judgements. Forgiveness is necessary for healing. It allows us not to lose sight of the other person's humanity. We have a need to take responsibility for past actions and then to forgive ourselves. Prayer and support, for the Christian, are ways of reaching self-forgiveness.

The Christian has to forgive in order to be in full contact with God. The Bible states very clearly what has to be done in order to receive God's forgiveness. It is as simple as it is profound: it demands that people repent of their sins and ask God to forgive them (Luke 24:47). Within the Christian faith, only the truly forgiven can be forgiving. Those who have experienced God's forgiveness are expected to forgive others wholeheartedly (Luke 6:37; Colossians 3:13). The motivation to forgive for a practising Christian will, therefore, have a fundamentally different value base to that of a non-Christian or a non-practising Christian. There is a real need for the client to understand from where their true motivation for forgiveness comes.

Forgiveness can offer an overwhelming sense of peace: 'Peace I leave with you, my peace I give unto you' (John 14:27). Applying the principles of forgiveness and reconciliation to personal and professional life relationships is crucial as, I believe, it opens the person to happiness, better health and a better life: it lessens depression and dissipates anger, enabling improved communication.

The influence of other Christians

Father Jenco was held captive for 564 days in makeshift prisons by the Shiite Muslims. He unconditionally forgave his captors while he was imprisoned. He had written a letter to this effect prior to knowing that there was any possibility of release. One of his captors read Jenco's letter and several months later asked his forgiveness using the words from his unsent letter: 'I was called to forgive, to let go revenge, retaliation, and vindictiveness. And I was challenged to forgive him [one of his captors] unconditionally. I could not forgive him on condition that he changed his behaviour to conform to my wishes and values. I had no control over his response' (Jenco 1993: 49). He forgave his captor. Jenco's forgiveness gave them permission to change and he was later freed. I believe, and this is central to the Christian view, that forgiveness does not depend on the repentance of the other person. The reverse may well be true: forgiveness can lead to repentance.

Being a Christian does not make forgiveness any easier. Corrie ten Boom wrote of being faced by one of her former SS guards from the Ravensbruck concentration camp where she and her sister had been sent for harbouring Jews – her sister had died in the camp. She had just finished preaching at a church service when the ex-guard came forward. After beaming and bowing, 'How grateful I am for your message *Fräulein*' he said, 'to think that, as you say, He has washed my sins away' (1971: 221). He told her that he had become a Christian and he thrust his hand forward to shake hers, seeking her forgiveness as God had forgiven him. She wrote that her heart sank and she kept her hand by her side. She could not respond, as the memories of Ravensbruck came flooding back. While anger and vengeful thoughts boiled through her, she saw the sin of them. She prayed for God's forgiveness towards her and for His help in forgiving the guard. She could not feel anything, not even the slightest spark of warmth. Again she prayed a silent prayer asking Jesus to give her His forgiveness. Note the way in which forgiveness had to be an act of her will. As she felt able to take his hand, she felt in her heart a love and warmth which seemed to flood her whole being, bringing tears to her eyes.

I will offer one final example which readers may recall. In India, in 1999, a father and his two young sons, who were attending an annual Christian retreat, were burned to death by Hindu extremists while they were sleeping in the back of their van. People were prevented from rescuing them by the same extremists. For his wife, the mother of the boys, it was the knowledge of God and the strength that He gave her that helped her to forgive those who had carried out the attack. She prayed, at her family's funeral, that the killers would be touched by the love of Jesus and seek his forgiveness. Today, having forgiven these killers, healing has come into her life and she has been able to move on. She is currently realising her late husband's dream by running a small leprosy mission in India.

I believe it is possible to find freedom in forgiveness. However, I agree with the words of Nelson (2000: 35): 'Forgiveness means letting go of a certain kind of attachment to the perpetrator. Forgiveness hurts, too, because to forgive means to remember, and that often entails re-experiencing the hurt associated with the past'. Old hurts can be re-stimulated and feel raw and like new again. Finding new ways of being healthy is not easy, especially when someone has hurt you. One of the many joys of being a Christian is the knowledge that you are truly loved and that this love is unconditional. This is that basis of my way of thinking and being. And fundamental to this is the knowledge that I am able to forgive and be forgiven. For me, my faith is most helpful. However, I am aware that non-Christians may have other forms of self-support and certainly have a similar capacity for healing.

We need to work towards forgiveness

Unforgivingness is one of the strongest holds that occurs in people's lives. It can grow undetected inside, like a cancer eating away at the guts of its victim. It is an enemy. McMaster, in 'Thought for the Day' (9 August 2002), on BBC Radio 4, suggested that people become prisoners of the past due to their lack of insight and inability to find forgiveness. People who have survived major traumatic events such as a 11 September 2001, the Holocaust, an air crash, can find it hard to forgive themselves for surviving when so many have not. They can find it hard to forgive people who have caused such hurt and pain and may want to get their own back on those who have killed loved ones. I was struck by the words of the American chaplain in London when he was interviewed on the evening of 11 September on Premier Radio. He said (at a time when his son was still missing) that, unless we can forgive, we will be like the perpetrators of the attack.

Perhaps it is time for all of us to start dismantling our defensive walls of rage, hate and lack of knowledge. There is much to be gained from making forgiveness a goal in all things we do rather than holding onto our hurts in an unhealthy manner. Desmond Tutu knew what it was like to live in a society dominated by racism and oppression. As the head of the Truth and Reconciliation Commission (TRC) set up to encourage reconciliation between the former victims and their oppressors, he said:

> It is not enough to let bygones be bygones, indeed just saying that ensures it will not be so. Reconciliation does not come easy. Believing it does not ensure that it will ever be. We have to work and look the beast firmly in the eyes. Ultimately you discover that without forgiveness, there is no future.
>
> (Greer 1998)

Tutu believed that through injustice and oppression, victims can lose their personal dignity and sense of worth, and that the pain that had to be addressed in South Africa could not be solved through amnesia or denial. Tutu helped in the attempt to create conditions in which people could hear one another and, if possible, forgive so that there could be closure rather than the never-ending cycle of hatred. Forgiveness does not mean condoning terrible acts. For me, it is not impractical, idealistic nor impossible to achieve. It is thoroughly realistic. Unless I forgive, I do not believe it is possible to move on. To forgive is to let go.

The role of the therapist

The task of the therapist is to work alongside the client and make a journey of discovery with him or her in order that the person can discover how to live a more fulfilled life. The first step is the creation of a good therapeutic alliance in order that there is sufficient trust and safety for the client to feel able to begin to explore his or her concerns. A working alliance does not necessarily mean that my clients raise issues of forgiveness or an inability to forgive. For me, the challenge is to be available, if this is important to them.

As the therapeutic alliance develops, our clients' stories unfold, as does their ability to share their feelings of hurt, bitterness, shame and other negative emotions. I find Rogers' (1961) core conditions of unconditional positive regard, genuineness and empathy crucial in developing a trusting relationship with clients. This helps me keep in contact with the client and his or her story.

Where the first goal is forgiveness

For some people, their presenting issue is their wish to forgive. Where individuals come to therapy with this as a goal, I clarify with them what they mean by forgiveness and, if they have a religious faith, how this links. I am interested in how unforgivingness was impacting on their lives, their relationships and way of being in the world. And as part of the assessment, I often explore whether part of their functioning is to please people and how well they can assert their own choices. This helps in the clarification of whether they are coming with the goal of forgiveness from an adult place or from the 'oughts' of an adapted child (Berne 1972). From these discussions, we can begin to make a contract.

Ruth, a Christian, came to me because I was a Christian therapist, saying she lacked self-confidence and had poor self-esteem. Her goal was to forgive. She had tried hard to do this, but without success. She wanted so badly to forgive because that was 'what you do as a believer'. There were a great number of 'oughts' and 'shoulds' in Ruth's use of language. When we explored her family background, it became clear that she had been much criticised as a child and had a punitive understanding of church life. What Ruth appeared not to have experienced from her family or church was empathy and unconditional positive regard.

I believed that Ruth was not ready to forgive, and yet respected that, for her as a Christian, this was what she wanted and needed to do. I was able to offer her the reassurance that God knew what was in her heart, He knew that she wanted to forgive. It was, therefore, all right to take her time getting to this place.

When a person has been badly hurt, they need, as Herman (1992) suggests, a chance to get in touch with the traumatic situation and re-experience the trauma. I was aware that Ruth needed space to fully acknowledge the abuse she had suffered and explore the profound impact this had had on her life. In trying to jump to forgiveness, she had missed a very important step.

Gradually she felt able to acknowledge the depth of her pain and anger. For Ruth, the first step was to address the trauma and to fully experience the feelings attached to it. Only then could she begin to consider forgiveness.

Other clients, as the therapeutic relationship builds, discover that they are blocked by anger and bitterness. If they are practising Christians, I will actively remind them that unforgivingness has to be addressed as part of their commitment to having a personal relationship with Jesus. I will start with a gentle challenge from a biblical framework, reminding them of the Lord's Prayer, 'Forgive us our trespasses as we forgive those who trespass against us' (Mathew 6:12). This acts as a reminder of their faith beliefs and where forgiveness fits. In making this suggestion, I need to be mindful that I could become another critical voice and re-stimulate a negative reaction in the client. So how can I challenge a client's beliefs without provoking shame or anger? Often with very great difficulty. This is where I find person-centred thinking most helpful. Rogers (1980) writes of gentle challenge and confrontation in order to enable clients to take responsibility for themselves. I find when I am able to work empathically with clients they are more able to hear the challenges that I may make. Then from a place of insight, choices can be made and new growth can occur.

With non-Christians, or those Christians with different beliefs, my approach will be different. There will still be the need for space to experience the feelings related to the wrongdoing. However, where the anger persists, I will be more tentative and focus initially on what is keeping the client in an apparently unhealthy place. I may question whether there is an issue around forgiveness, but I must wait to see whether he or she finds this relevant. I seek to use the language and goals as expressed by my clients.

I set out below a framework I find useful in thinking about working towards forgiveness. The model can be adapted for use with a goal such as reconciliation or letting go. However, I suggest that before therapists embark on work in this area, they think through their own attitudes towards forgiveness and what words such as 'reconciliation' or 'letting go' mean to them. They are then in a better position to consciously put this on one side in order to listen to what the terms mean to their clients. They also need to recognise their own struggle with forgiveness of themselves and others, as they may then have more understanding of, and empathy for, their clients' struggles.

A framework for working towards forgiveness

- **Recognise**. Help clients recognise the impact negative feelings such as bitterness are having on their lives.
- **Challenge**. Gently challenge the impact unforgivingness is having on their lives and what forgiveness might be like.
- **Power**. Help clients become aware of their power to let go and the power that comes from letting go.
- **Discrepancy**. Encourage clients to stay with the discrepancy between the cost of unforgivingness and forgiveness to the point where they make the decision to forgive or to move on in some other way.

Recognise

I have written of the importance for clients to have space to share their distress and anger when they have been badly treated. However, when they appear stuck, and their life is affected by bitterness, I encourage clients to stand back and look at what is happening to them.

I worked for some months with James, aware how embittered he appeared to be without knowing why. Finally he told me about a turbulent relationship he had for ten years before becoming a Christian. His then partner, Martha, had, at times, been violent towards him and he had felt unable to stop the violence or leave. While Martha was making secret plans to leave, she stole more than a thousand pounds from him. James had felt unable to talk about this because he had felt so ashamed at being duped. He couldn't forgive himself for entering into a relationship with Martha in the first place and at, what he saw, as his own stupidity in putting up with the abuse. He kept talking about how stupid he was. I was puzzled and asked him where this came from. James recognised that, as a child growing up, he had been constantly put down. The only way he had pleased his parents was when he did well at school. James still felt very hurt and angry towards Martha. Though it was five years before, he was aware that he had not felt able to trust anyone else since that time.

Challenge

This is the point at which I am likely to use the words 'unforgivingness' and 'forgiveness' for the first time. I encourage clients
to explore the notion of forgiveness and what impact forgiving
might have on their lives. I will then ask them to contrast this with
their current state of unforgivingness. However, it is important
to be aware that the client may so lack self-esteem and self-
confidence, that he or she may find it hard to imagine being in a
different place.

James admitted he felt really ashamed: 'You must think I'm really
stupid.' He felt a fool as he knew how badly Martha had behaved in
previous relationships. Yet he'd been willing to do anything to keep
her. James did not turn up for the next two sessions.

Durham (2000) warns that 'exploited repressive patients' may
prematurely terminate therapy due to feeling the devastating
impact of shame as they begin to realise the extent to which they
have been misused by parents and others. This may impact on the
transference, with the client assuming that the therapist will have
no respect for someone who has put up with being abused. Or the
person may devalue the therapeutic relationship and any hint that
there is another way of being in the world. This phase of therapy is
often slow and painful.

When he returned, I gently challenged James: 'I am wondering
how your life would be, if you were to forgive yourself and Martha
for what happened?' James got angry. He said that was a stupid
idea. How could he ever forgive? However, the next week, he said
he had been thinking and praying about what I had said. He had
spent five years feeling furious with Martha and feeling furious
with himself. He was aware how critical he had become and found
it hard to imagine how this could change. Yet he knew he wanted
to move beyond a place of such bitterness.

Power

Many clients have little belief in their ability to change. They
experience themselves as coming from an 'I'm not OK' position
(Berne 1972): shame and an absence of self-forgiveness impacts in a
way oppressors could never, on their own, have achieved.

An empathic therapeutic relationship is crucial in helping clients
find their own self-belief and from this position a greater sense of

power. The relationship offers a space in which the person does not feel so alone and isolated, feels supported by the therapist's belief that change is possible. I often ask clients what would help them find their strength. If the client is a practising Christian, I might ask how God fits into this.

At times, the client will want to develop strategies to support themselves when they feel anxious. Sometimes teaching the client assertiveness skills can enable them to feel empowered. I find an adaptation I have made of the transactional analysis (TA) model, 'permission, protection and potency' (Berne 1972) helpful in thinking about my work, particularly in relation to self-forgiveness. Clients may well need to feel they have *permission* to judge themselves less harshly; *protection* from negative judgement within the therapeutic relationship and a belief in the therapist's *potency* to help them counteract persecutory introjects as they begin to feel more compassion for themselves.

Just before the next session, James phoned and said, 'Look, I can't do it. I don't think there's any point coming back. You must think I'm so foolish.' I told him that was not my experience of him. I invited him to reconsider, to pray and said that I would keep the session open for him. I also prayed for him. He came to the session and said he was relieved when I had said I hadn't experienced him as stupid. He had prayed and recognised he had been in a stuck place for a long time. He said it was time for him to stop running and face the past.

Discrepancy

At this stage in the process, the client may well feel at an impasse, have a desire to forgive and yet harbour doubts and fears about forgiving. The client needs continued empathic attunement as he or she struggles with the dilemma, and the therapist needs to be sensitive to the client's pace.

James began to believe that I was not going to judge him and to develop some compassion for himself and the mistakes he had made. He realised that he was now very different from the young man who had fallen in love with Martha. He was aware how difficult it still was to forgive Martha and how he continued to hold back from getting involved in other relationships. Gradually, his humility in owning his part in what had occurred helped him begin to consider the possibility of forgiving her. He thought of times when he had hurt others, through insensitive, misguided intentions or malicious acts. This enabled him to place his emotional injuries into context. As a Christian, James knew that part of his faith involved him forgiving Martha and that he had to resolve the faith issues between God and himself. He did this by prayer, both in the therapy sessions and outside.

There is no neat and tidy movement towards forgiveness. Clients inevitably move back and forth between stages. Considering forgiveness, as Nelson (2000) said, can often re-stimulate old wounds and the pain will be re-evoked.

James spent time sharing his distress and anger at how he had been treated by Martha – and his parents too. Some months later he said that, while he could not condone what Martha had done to him, he now felt ready to forgive and let go.

Forgiveness and the non-Christian

I have given two examples – Ruth and James – both of whom are practising Christians and where the client and I had a similar value base. Mark did not have either a faith or religious belief.

He came to therapy as part of course requirements and it took some time before he admitted the extent of the anger he felt towards his father who had been emotionally and physically abusive to him during his childhood. He was preoccupied with fantasies of revenge. In our work together he spoke in considerable detail about the abuse he had experienced as a child. While, occasionally, he would become sad, he primarily felt anger and bitterness at the way he had been treated.

Mark said that he would never stop feeling bitter for what had been done to him. I encouraged him to stand back and look at the impact his feelings were having on his life. He recognised he had a great deal of anger and resentment towards others, tied in with distrust. As therapy progressed, I challenged him to discuss the impact of unforgivingness and what forgiveness, or letting go, might be like. First we looked at the impact of unforgivingness. He admitted, for the first time, that his angry outbursts were causing havoc in his marriage and his wife was threatening to leave. 'And what about forgiveness?' I asked. Mark began to muse on the idea. His father was dead and he knew it was impossible to successfully retaliate. There is a word in Hebrew, 'yetzer', meaning 'inclination' or 'imagination' (Montefiore and Loewe 1974). In Rabbinical

Judaism, there are two *yetzers*, one which signifies the propensity for good and the other for evil. I shared the notion of positive or negative inclinations with Mark and he immediately identified his father as being selfish and aggressive and enjoying seeing him miserable. This prompted him to discuss how much of his father he had taken on board. He became quite tearful as he realised how defensive he had become: 'Listen, I know from all this training that I'm covering up how sad I really feel!'

In this instance, I thought it might be useful to use the therapeutic technique of 'the two chairs' (Houston 1982) with Mark to help him separate out the two sets of feelings in order to give expression to both the angry and the hurt parts of himself. I described the process to Mark and we contracted to do the work. I suggested that he put his anger on one chair, as it were, and speak metaphorically from his hurting self. When he did this he became very distressed and realised how hurt he felt. When he spoke from his angry self, he found it did not have the same impact on him.

My experience with two-chair work is that it is very powerful. Clients discover words, views, feelings and attitudes that they have not expected or experienced before. Mark gained an understanding of the extent to which he had used anger as a way of protecting himself from hurt and that he had introjected his father's feelings and attitudes as if they were his own. Over the next period in therapy he faced his distress. He was gradually able to separate out from the negative experience and see it in a different light. I suggested that he write a letter to his father with as much of the anger, hurt and pain as he wanted to express in order to begin the process of release. My experience is that this can help the client feel more powerful and in control.

As English was not his first language, Mark decided to write the letter in his language of origin. He wrote it at home and brought it to the next session. I was there as a witness, to listen even though I could not understand the words. Here all my understanding of his non-verbal communication was to be tested. I needed to be aware of intonations, tones, gestures, pace. This allowed me to ask for clarification on what was happening at different points in the letter-reading.

Expressing the extent of his anger and hurt helped Mark make some movement towards letting go of his bitterness. It was a slow and difficult process. I had to follow my client's direction and follow him in the process. Forgiveness is not a word he used in relation to his father, but he has spoken of feeling able to forgive himself for having been so harsh towards others and that has helped him contemplate letting go and moving forward.

Herman (1992) writes that trauma is only resolved when the survivor develops a new mental 'schema' or map for understanding what happened. Mark was deeply impacted by seeing his father's anger in himself and then by realising how much he used anger to protect himself against pain. The shift that Mark was able to make in his perception of himself was I feel due to his confidence and willingness to change and to move forward in his therapeutic process.

Self-forgiveness

Rowe writes that 'we cannot forgive ourselves unless we forgive others and we cannot forgive others unless we forgive ourselves' (1991: 266). It is quite amazing how forgiveness can calm a sea of hurts. It is difficult, but very important, to grasp the concept of self-forgiveness. When working with people who have survived a major life trauma, there is often a sense of self-blame, sometimes due to a lack of self-worth. As an example, how many adult survivors of childhood abuse are left with a sense that they should have done something different? ('I should have told my mother', 'I deserved what happened to me', 'It was my fault'.) This so often links with their inability to stop blaming themselves. Logically, as there was no sense of moral responsibility, there is no need for self-forgiveness. However, on an emotional level, people often have the need to forgive themselves for the 'if onlys' and to forgive themselves for the impact bitterness and regret have had on their subsequent lives.

So often wrongs are perpetrated by two people. In terms of Karpman's Drama Triangle (1968), the victim can become the persecutor. (It's all your fault; if it weren't for you; why don't you change?) Or the person is a victim in one context and so consumed with rage that they take it out on other people, thus becoming a persecutor somewhere else. The first step in self-forgiveness is taking responsibility for our actions, facing them and admitting we were wrong. For the Christian, it is about embracing the aspect of the Lord's Prayer, 'Forgive us our debts as we forgive our debtors' (Mathew 6:14). Belief in God's forgiveness can free us to forgive ourselves. For believers and non-believers, self-forgiveness involves being able to say 'I have learned from this, I can make reparation and be different'. The very act of truly repenting is one that results in a life-changing reaction. From this, self-forgiveness can follow.

When we think to forgive others, the first step must still be taking responsibility for any wrongdoing of our own. Then, even if they don't accept our forgiveness, the fact that we have forgiven them releases us. It does not allow bitterness, hurt and pain to remain. I believe that if we harbour a grudge then it will eventually eat us up. People become critical of themselves as well as others. They may well damage themselves more that the other person. While therapists may be more used to thinking of the impact of unforgivingness – of bitterness and self criticism – on a person's emotions, Thoresen *et al.* (2000) suggest there may also be an indirect link between forgiveness and physical health.

Loss and forgiveness

I find it helpful to link forgiveness with the classical stages of loss and grief. I have found that once clients have worked through feelings of grief for the wrong they have suffered, they can begin to move on. Kubler-Ross (1969) identified five stages in grief: denial and isolation; anger; bargaining; depression; and acceptance. I would suggest that forgiveness of both self and others finds its natural place when depression has passed and before acceptance is achieved. There needs to be a mental decision to forgive oneself or another. This is not possible when self-esteem and confidence is low – the person needs to reach the point where he or she feels strong enough to forgive.

Conclusion

> So watch yourselves. If your brother sins, rebuke him, and if he repents, forgive him. If he sins against you seven times in a day, and seven times comes back to you and says, 'I repent,' forgive him.
>
> (Luke 17:3–4)

Forgiveness does not mean ignoring the wrong things people do or condoning them; it is about seeing the humanity in ourselves and other people and giving ourselves and others the opportunity to change.

Forgiveness is an active act of will that allows harmonious relationships to be resumed. Is it really possible for us as counsellors and psychotherapists to work with clients towards forgiveness if we ourselves still hold unforgivingness in our hearts? I believe that something will be missing within the therapeutic alliance unless we are prepared to acknowledge our own issues to ourselves. I know the pitfalls that I face. I am a person with all the same vulnerabilities as my clients. I need to hold onto my belief and keep my faith active and strong.

Forgiveness offers freedom and a quality of life which can never be achieved while we hold onto anger and bitterness. Not entering into the freedom which forgiveness brings can mean the difference between having a rich life of awareness or always having a sense that there is something missing from life. What is important is to be acutely aware of the connections between forgiveness, religion and well-being.

In the words of Desmond Tutu, 'We can indeed transcend the conflicts of the past, we can hold hands as we realise our common humanity. Without forgiveness there would be no future' (Greer 1998).

References

Berne, E. (1972) *What Do You Say After You Say Hello?* London: Corgi.

Boom ten, C. (1971) *The Hiding Place.* London: Hodder & Stoughton.

Durham, M.S. (2000) *The Therapist's Encounters With Revenge and Forgiveness.* London: Jessica Kingsley.

Greer, C. (1998) The world is hungry for goodness, www.forgiveness-day.org/tutu.htm.

Herman, J.L. (1992) *Trauma and Recovery.* London: HarperCollins.

Houston, G. (1982) *The Red Book Of Gestalt.* London: The Rochester Foundation.

Jenco, L.M. (1993) *Bound to Forgive: Pilgrimages in Time and Mind.* Notre Dame: Ave Maria Press.

Karpman, S. (1968) Fairy tales and script drama analysis, *Transactional Analysis Bulletin*, 7(26): 39–44.

Kubler-Ross, E. (1969) *On Death and Dying.* New York: Macmillan.

McCullough, M.E. and Worthington, E.L. (1999) Religion and the forgiving personality, *Journal of Personality*, 67: 6.

Montefiore, C.G. and Loewe, H. (1974) *A Rabbinic Anthology*. New York: Schocken Books.

Nelson, B.M. (2000) *The Unburdened Heart: Five Keys To Forgiveness and Freedom*. San Francisco: HarperCollins.

Rowe D. (1991) *The Courage to Live*. London: HarperCollins.

Rogers, C.R. (1961) *On Becoming a Person*. London: Constable.

Rogers, C.R. (1980) *A Way Of Being*. Boston, MA: Houghton Mifflin.

Thoresen, C.E., Harris, A.S. and Luskin, F. (2000) Forgiveness and health: an unanswered question, in M.E. McCullough, K.I. Pargament and C.E. Thoresen, *Forgiveness, Theory, Research and Practice*. New York: The Guilford Press.

Thorne, B. (1992) *Carl Rogers*. London: Sage.

Chapter 3

Be cautious about forgiveness

Cynthia Ransley

> Understand, and forgive. It is what my mother taught me to do,
> poor patient gentle Christian soul . . . Understand, and forgive . . .
> and the effort has quite exhausted me. I could do with some
> anger to energise me, and bring me back to life again. But where
> can I find that anger? Who is to help me?
>
> (Weldon 1975: 1–2)

More than 25 years ago, my partner and I decided against the
expected religious ceremony and married in a registry office. At the
reception afterwards, a family friend came up to me and said,
'Cynthia, I want you to know that I will forgive you, whatever you
do.' My response, 'Thank you,' still rings in my ears.

I have no doubt that she meant to be kind. But the religious
belief system which lay behind her words was one of certainty, of
right and wrong. And, although I was no longer a member of her
faith, for that moment I found myself accepting her truth and
absolution. It was only much later that I felt indignant.

The lesson I learnt was to be cautious about forgiveness. Be
cautious about the motivation which lies behind the wish to forgive, be cautious for the client who comes wanting help to forgive
and be cautious, above all, about the word itself. Forgiveness
may carry too much conflicting emotional baggage. 'Accepting',
'becoming reconciled', 'letting go' and 'closure' may be more
appropriate words in our more secular society. Whatever the word,
hurt, anger, regret, the desire for revenge must be faced.

After a wrongdoing or a tragedy, most people struggle to come
to terms with what has happened. Talk of forgiveness, at this stage,
may be quite inappropriate – in fact they may be better off not

forgiving. I will explore these issues by referring to feedback I received from over 100 therapists and social workers who attended workshops or completed questionnaires. I will draw case examples from work and unpublished research I have been doing with people bereaved as a result of a medical accident, usually involved in a complaints procedure or litigation.

Background

When the co-editor, Terri Spy, and I came together to talk and write about forgiveness, as we said in the Introduction, we were immediately aware how fundamentally different our views were. It took time to realise that our clients also presented differently. Regularly, clients talked with her of forgiveness, while my clients rarely used the term with me. This may be because some clients are drawn to Spy because of her Christian views, but perhaps my ambivalence towards forgiveness influenced the process.

Given the disparity between us, I thought it important to harness the views of other therapists in Britain, and I did this via workshops attended by some 40 therapists (psychotherapists and counsellors) and a questionnaire which was completed by a further 76 therapists and social workers: some were qualified, the rest in training. While they came from different training institutes, the predominant orientation of the therapists was integrative. The findings may have been different had the sample come from those working within, for example, a psychoanalytic or cognitive-behavioural frame. However, there was little difference in the response between the therapists and social workers.

Is there any correlation between religious affiliation and attitude towards forgiveness? Forty-two per cent of the therapists described themselves as having what might be termed traditional religious beliefs, and of these twenty-five identified themselves as Christian: this included eight Catholics, two Church of England, one Quaker and one Greek Orthodox. Three respondents were Jewish, one Muslim and three Hindu. A further two described themselves as pagan and 'goddess/earth religion'.

This left 40 people (58 per cent) who did not see themselves as having religious beliefs. Almost half gave details of spiritual and humanist beliefs – including a Buddhist – such as a belief in the interconnectedness of all life, an absolute belief in the life of the spirit and the sacredness of the natural.

This finding contrasts sharply with two American studies of therapists' attitudes to forgiveness (DiBlasio 1993: DiBlasio and Proctor 1993). In these, only 8 to 10 per cent of respondents had no religious preference, whereas here the majority saw themselves in this category. The therapists in this study had a far wider variation in attitude towards forgiveness than in the American studies. While the numbers surveyed were small, it may be worth bearing this in mind when looking at some of the American literature.

The low level of religious affiliation among therapists may warrant further research given the difference with the recent UK national census (2001) in which more than 75 per cent of respondents described themselves as having a religious affiliation.

Thoughts on forgiveness

Therapists need to be aware that the word 'forgiveness' is perceived very differently by people. This showed starkly in my research where a good number gave, as their gut reaction to the term, words like 'softness', 'compassion', 'peace', 'release' and 'an image of a muddy river flowing and flowing until it becomes clear'. And just as many among the non-Christian groups gave negative words as a response: 'cynical', 'repulsion', 'dubious Christian notion', 'a requirement of the pious', 'no such thing' and 'yuk'. For one, the first feeling was panic: 'I always equate it with the giving over of some important part of myself which has been hurt, can never be reclaimed and will always be thrashed'.

The reasons for the negativity were linked to power and the potential for the misuse of power. Bestowing forgiveness (note the patronising nature of the phrase) can be a passive aggressive act, an indirect way of showing disdain, even revenge – without expressing the feelings directly. Several wrote of the power forgiveness bestowed on the forgiver, the potential for projecting the blame. One wrote, 'I dislike the word forgiveness, it smacks of taking the moral high ground. Most of life's a muddle, rights and wrongs on both sides'. And, as in the example of my wedding, a few respondents wrote of situations where they had been forgiven for wrongs which, in their code, were not wrong at all! The danger of feeling judged by the other from, in the terms of transactional analysis (TA), an 'I'm OK, you're not OK' position' (Berne 1972) is strong.

Some of the negativity stemmed from childhood memories of a religion they no longer practised: 'the humiliation of confession', wrote one. Forgiveness in these terms was synonymous with religious expectations of sin, of 'oughts' from a culture with which they no longer identified, perhaps even did not respect. Respondents included such biblical references as, 'Turn the other cheek', 'Love your enemies as yourself' and 'Forgive us our trespasses as we forgive those who trespass against us'. For some, they served as an inspiration, for others they inspired disquiet.

Several wrote of their concern that the client may feel compelled to forgive and that it is important to assess, with the client, whether she or he is coming from, in TA terms, an Adapted Child position (Berne 1972) – replaying childhood behaviours, feelings or thoughts – or an adult place of reasoning. The injunctions may be familial rather than religious or cultural. One wrote: 'As a child, I was always told to be a good girl and I know I still want to do the right thing and forgive'. How many parents have pushed their older child to 'make up' after a fight with 'You're the older one, don't be angry any more'. There may be gender and other cultural variations in the expectation that the child will understand and forgive, as there were for Chloe in Fay Weldon's *Female Friends* (1975), quoted at the beginning of this chapter. The pressure to deny feelings of anger and resentment, to move straight on to forgiveness and reconciliation can be strong. One therapist responded in the questionnaire, 'Sometimes, I feel I am going through the motions; dig down deep and I have not forgiven because my pain was unbearable'.

A few remembered instances where they had found a mutual expression of forgiveness, healing and a way of both making peace with the other. Several parents noted that the one person to whom they said 'I forgive you' was their child after a transgression or accident. I can only hypothesise the reason why the expression seemed to be more used with children. It may reflect many being more able to love their children regardless. Perhaps the parents had some distant memory of the words being said to them as children. It may also reflect the interdependency in the parent-child relationship: the parent's sense of responsibility for the actions of their child and the wish to model constructive behaviour which can bring closure.

This assumes a relationship in which there is a dialogue about the disagreement or wrongdoing, perhaps even acceptance of mutual wrongdoing. However, often, even when the hurt is within a personal relationship, it is not possible to talk to the other about it. He or she may no longer be alive, be unwilling to talk or may not accept that she has wronged the other. Or the victim may fear raising the issue. One wrote, in the questionnaire, that forgiveness need not involve another person: 'It's an internal process of moving on, of letting go of deeply felt anger and a sense of injustice'. This links with the view expressed by several that what was important, at the receiving end, was not being verbally forgiven but experiencing a change of attitude: 'actions speak louder than words'.

It seems, from the research, that most often the expression is only used over minor issues or in a light-hearted way: a half joking 'I forgive you' sometimes with the barbed caveat 'thousands wouldn't!' I am reminded of the TA 'gallows laugh' (Berne 1972), a way of making light of something hurtful. Being open with the other about wrongs within a relationship, talking about feelings, getting to the point where there can be talk of forgiveness: for many, this becomes too scary, too intimate and laughter may offer some relief from tension.

Obviously, it is a problem that, in our more secular society, the word forgiveness is too bound up with religion. Only two respondents with a religious faith expressed doubts about the term. The doubts and, at times, abhorrence, came from many without a religious faith. And the majority, whether they had a religious faith or not, tended to use other expressions to someone who had wronged or hurt them: 'Let's put it behind us and move on'; 'Let's forget it'; 'Let's begin again'. Note the way the wrong or problem has become the depersonalised 'it'. This is quite different from the direct 'I forgive you'. No one offered a phrase which included 'I' (such as 'I'm willing to forget it') – the nearest was 'It's all right'.

In the questionnaire, I asked whether there was a word or phrase respondents used to denote putting a wrong behind them. The words most commonly used were 'acceptance', 'becoming reconciled' and 'letting go'. I prefer the words to end in 'ing': accept*ing*, becom*ing* reconciled, lett*ing* go, to be clear that we are talking about a process rather than an event. Even where people feel they have put a hurt behind them, say a partner's sexual transgression, the feelings may be reactivated by his or her becoming friendly with another, putting on weight and feeling less attractive, or others finding out what happened – the impact of the affair having a public not just a purely private dimension.

This has been very apparent in my involvement with people bereaved after a medical accident. The notion that there is a discrete stage of 'acceptance' or 'forgiveness' is quickly disabused. As one said, 'Just when I am beginning to accept what has happened and grieve for my husband, a brown envelope comes through the door [from a lawyer or the health service]. I feel the fear of "what's in it?" and then more fury that I am no nearer the truth'.

To what extent are terms such as 'letting go' simply the twenty-first-century secular equivalent of forgiveness? I will continue with the definition I used in Chapter 1. Enright and the Human Development Study Group define forgiving as: 'a willingness to abandon one's right to resentment, negative judgment and indifferent behavior toward one who unjustly hurt us, while fostering the undeserved qualities of compassion, generosity, and even love toward him or her' (Enright *et al.* 1998: 46–7). There are several crucial aspects to this definition. First, the person recognises he or she has been deeply and unjustly hurt. The person affected is willing to let go of negative feelings, negative thoughts and negative behaviours towards the other – not only giving up overtly hostile behaviours but also the more subtle, indifferent responses. Forgiving, here, also involves offering care, kindness, even love to the other. This suggests offering a relationship with the other either in reality or in the mind.

A number of respondents, who valued the notion of forgiveness, made comments that echoed this definition. One wrote that the word carries absolution, a sense of completion that other words fail to carry. I found 'making peace with oneself regarding another' helpful in the emphasis placed first on the peace needed within ourselves before we can move outwards. Another wrote that forgiveness had finally taken place 'at the end of a long process of understanding, reparation and realisation that if the relationship was to continue I had to let go, learn to trust and love again'.

The confusing result of the research is that, to some extent, people use expressions such as 'forgiveness', 'letting go', 'becoming reconciled' and 'acceptance' interchangeably. The latter three may be more generally acceptable terms as they are value-free. For some people forgiveness has the additional quality of offering love to the other but another may use the term 'acceptance' with exactly the same intent. As we let go of feelings of anger and hurt we may begin to feel understanding and compassion towards the other – or our compassion towards the other may help us let go of our anger and hurt. Therapists, clearly, must check exactly what a client means by any term used, and help the client hold onto their reasoning capacities in the work. Feeling compassion towards another, or not being caught up in bitterness or resentment, is different from condoning a wrong and agreeing to a reconciliation with someone who is violent and unwilling or unable to change.

Justice and revenge

There seemed to be an agreement among respondents, whether they were in favour of the term forgiveness or not, that holding onto bitterness, resentment or a grudge is debilitating. One respondent wrote: 'it [bitterness] will eat away at you and at all relationships and prevent you from leading life to the full'. Another wrote that it is vital we become aware of our wish to punish, our need to stay attached to a negative object as this obstructs our energy.

However, it is natural to feel anger in the face of an injustice. As one said, 'Anger can energise and be a powerful motivator for change'. Baures (1996) writes that the ability to feel the fury of hate can be a healthy and important part of the recovery process, as it lessens feelings of powerlessness and self-blame – but only if the person can, in time, let it go.

Some individuals cannot. They become stuck, going over and over what has happened. As Steiner (1993) puts it, they also become preoccupied with the future: a future where right will be done and they will be avenged. On a psychological level, as I suggested in Chapter 1, there is a fine line between the desire for revenge and the desire for justice – also a preoccupation with a future where right will be done, but here the emphasis is on the wrong never taking place again – either to them or another.

Society benefits from those who devote themselves to the pursuit of justice, manage to discover the truth and bring the guilty to trial. It is the archetypal film where the good guy triumphs over adversity. A person may use the experience to set up a self-help group or seek changes in the law. For some, the quest for justice and prevention can be healing. For others, the need for justice or revenge can keep the person simultaneously stuck in the past – and in a fantasised future, the present being too awful to contemplate.

This was the case for a couple whom I will call Jane and David. Their only child, Alan, aged 12, became ill with a fever, severe headache and an intermittent rash. That night, while Jane was at work, the symptoms became more acute and David took Alan to the casualty department of the local hospital. During the examination, the doctor asked what school Alan went to. David gave him the name: it was a school for children with behavioural problems.

The doctor told David not to worry ('He could be putting it on') and sent Alan home. Alan died that night of meningitis. The doctor's comment remained rooted in David's memory: 'If only I'd said he went to Eton,' he said. 'He'd still be alive.' Whether true or not, that 'if only' would not go away. The parents tried to find out from the hospital what had gone wrong, whether the child would have died even if he hadn't been sent home. The hospital denied any liability. Jane and David mounted a negligence action that they were unable to prove. When I met them five years later they were still fighting, now trying to make sure other children would be safe from misdiagnosis.

A preoccupation with finding the truth, with justice, is one way of managing emptiness and depression, a way, Jane knew, of trying to keep Alan alive, of continuing to feel like a mother. It is also a way of managing desperate powerlessness. Jane and David's only child had died and they had been unable to prevent it. They felt keenly that they had lost out because of their rank. The name of the school had labelled Alan, he had a tattoo, David had arrived in grubby work clothes, he had told the receptionist he was worried about meningitis, but he hadn't liked to 'make a fuss' and say it to the doctor. What is important here is that this was their perception – at the point when their child had died, they experienced this further blow to their self-esteem. There was also a powerlessness in relation to the hospital staff who did not even say they were sorry Alan had died: 'They wouldn't, would they? They had paid a lot of money to train that young doctor, they wouldn't want to damage her career after that investment.'

David's anger towards the doctor alternated with guilt for giving the school's name and for taking Alan home. Jane's anger towards the doctor, and some towards her husband, alternated with guilt that she had not been there to protect her son – she had switched her mobile off, so did not hear the calls.

Relationships often do not survive such a tragedy. One may be consumed with grief, the other with seeking vengeance or justice and neither can support the other. Jane and David stayed united in their campaign, but they found it hard to focus on any other aspect of life. Their constant preoccupation with what had happened blocked them against fully experiencing their desperate sadness at their loss and interfered with the process of grieving.

Lampen (1994) reminds us that in the interests of social harmony, law-abiding citizens have voluntarily surrendered their rights of retaliation to the state. Think of the additional feelings of confusion and powerlessness when the state does nothing. I cite a medical accident, but this is equally the case for any person whose loved one has died at the hands of another. There may be no recourse to the law because of a technicality, or there may be a lack of money to pursue legal action, or the lawyer may be inexperienced. Society, on which we had depended, has failed us. Our safe, predictable world is torn apart.

Self-forgiveness

The area I wish I had highlighted more in the research questionnaire was self-forgiveness. A number of respondents included comments on it and I was able to make contact with a few of those who were the most vitriolic about the term 'forgiveness'.

From this, I can tentatively suggest that the term 'self-forgiveness' appears more generally acceptable and value-free. Several wrote that we have to learn to forgive ourselves if we are to have compassion towards another who has done us wrong. This can be true, but early critical messages we have internalised may primarily focus either on self, other or both. As one respondent put it, 'Forgiveness of self and others are currents in the same river, both hindered by the burden of resentment'.

Many readers will know people who find it easier to forgive others than themselves. In TA terms, self-blame reinforces the 'I'm not OK, you're OK' position (Berne 1972). Often, when people are abused, they blame themselves, becoming overwhelmed with guilt, self-hatred and shame.

Thurston (2000) and Dobbins (2000) write about working on issues of forgiveness and self-forgiveness. Thurston deals with evangelical and fundamentalist Protestants and Dobbins with Pentecostal Protestants. Thurston points to the struggle with perfectionism many clients from these faiths have, especially as they consider Jesus' admonition 'Be perfect, therefore as your heavenly Father is perfect' (Mathew 5:48).

For Dobbins, guilt is likely to be a key concern: guilt for transgressions for which they feel unable to forgive themselves and guilt over difficulties with forgiving others. He encourages clients to read scriptural passages related to God's forgiveness. If they can believe in God's forgiveness but still feel guilty, he will seek to challenge their belief that they can feel 'forgiven by God but condemned by one's self' with such questions as 'Is your conscience more difficult to satisfy than the holy nature of God?' (2000: 171).

Guilt and perfectionism are not the prerogative of conservative Protestants. Laura Davis is quite clear, in her work with people who have been sexually abused, that healing involves learning to forgive themselves. Forgiving the abuser is not necessary to health. She writes, 'If you're struggling with shame, you will need to forgive the child inside of you for having been so vulnerable, for having needed attention and affection. You'll have to forgive your adult self for the ways you coped, for the mistakes you've made' (1990: 334).

Developing self-compassion – the capacity to face shame, remorse and the desire for revenge and then develop the capacity to self-soothe – is hard. So hard, that, in my view, it is crucial to tackle any moral injunctions around forgiveness.

What makes it feasible to begin to move on? Fully facing the pain

In the questionnaire, I asked respondents what they considered was necessary for a person to move on. Over and over again, they pointed to the need to allow space and time to acknowledge the wrong, to face and experience the fullness of thoughts and the fullness of feelings about what has happened. As one wrote, 'We have a need to face the wrong/hurt in oneself fully and at all levels'. This will involve facing both feelings in relation to ourselves – grief, hurt, distress, shame, guilt – as well as feelings towards the wrongdoer, including anger, blame and the desire for revenge.

I believe we cannot get in touch fully with the feelings without facing what the loss or betrayal means to us. And it is this that makes me believe that grieving and letting go is a lengthy, sometimes never-ending, process, as it is only in the fullness of time that we can understand the implications of what has happened. The impact on how we view our self is likely to go beyond our relationship with the other, the wrongdoer. It may also affect our feelings of potency with other people, our ability to trust others. One respondent wrote: 'I cannot make much progress towards serenity of the spirit without reconciling myself to the past'. Yet that can be hard as a loss or betrayal is an inevitable challenge to our view of the world. Faith and spiritual beliefs may be, even temporarily, torn apart. Neimeyer and Anderson (2002) write of the need to make sense of a loss, and we may need to face the fact that there is no sense.

A wrong or loss brings us into a confrontation with, as Yalom (1980) puts it, the 'givens' of our existence: death, isolation, finding meaning in life and freedom. To these, I would add, a fifth given: inequality. We are unequal beings with unequal opportunities and luck. Many reading this book were born into a society where there was comparative peace and prosperity; others may have faced war and famine. Some are born into a loving family and others are abused. Some of us face death and illness at an early age, others do not. It is within this existential frame that I believe we can best understand our need to find ways of making sense of what has happened and ways of living with our history. For Holloway (2002: 43) this involves us actively saying 'yes to the tragic reality of life, including the facts of pain and loss [and] a wise, sometimes rueful awareness that the universe is bigger than us and will get us all in the end'.

In facing a traumatic wrongdoing, our sense of isolation is likely to be intensified and perhaps it is no surprise – especially as those who gave their views were largely therapists – that what many felt helped at this stage was to be able to express their feelings to another and to be heard and understood.

Is it a question of forgiveness?

Let us use the Enright definition (Enright *et al.* 1998) as a starting point and summarise forgiveness as letting go of negative judgement and feeling compassion towards the wrongdoer. I asked the question, 'Do you think it is important to forgive – either a person or group – in order to be able to move on or come to terms with what has happened?' The vast majority of respondents thought it was, though the focus was more often on letting go of anger and bitterness than developing compassion for the other. This included a number who did not care for the actual *term* forgiveness.

I did not ask if it was *essential* to forgive in order to move on. Despite this, around a third of the group made the comment that it is not necessary to forgive: it is possible to move on *despite* the other person. This was a sizeable number adding a comment which was not requested. What I take from this is that most of the respondents value the *ability* to let go of anger and bitterness, seeing it as important for personal well-being and necessary if personal and community relationships are to flourish. But, many believe, we can move on without developing compassion for the wrongdoer.

This would fit with Mary Baures' research. She interviewed 20 people, chosen because they had managed to make a positive life transformation after extreme trauma or loss. Some learned to forgive, some made a positive effort to alter negative thought processes. The defining constant was that they had not repressed their trauma. In contrast, all the survivors had 'revisited, reworked and transformed their horrible experiences in creative projects and through helping others' (1996: 88). On an equally adaptive note, several answering the questionnaire wrote that, while they had not forgiven someone who had wronged them, they had been able to let go of the feelings and move away, get on with life. How do people reach this point?

Where the wrong is acknowledged

Almost all who responded said that where the wrong was acknowledged they felt much more able to let go of feelings of anger and hurt. What is wanted is that the other accepts responsibility, acknowledges that she or he was wrong and apologises. Though several said this may suffice, one wrote that an apology was not enough: what he needed was for the person to 'stay around' to hear the impact the wrongdoing had had. Apologising again after listening, he felt, was more meaningful, as was checking to see whether there was anything else that might help, such as some kind of reparation.

In the literature on forgiveness, much is made of the importance of developing empathy *for* the wrongdoer. What we are discussing here is the need people have for understanding and empathy *from* the wrongdoer. This can be seen vividly in medical accidents. On the few occasions where the health worker has admitted a mistake, apologised and been compassionate, this has made an overwhelming difference. Often, there are mitigating circumstances for the health worker who may be working long hours, under considerable pressure. And, often enough, medical accidents are a systems failure where no one person can be blamed. An initial defensive response to an accident or an inadequate handling of the initial complaint can lead to an adversarial conflict in which both parties suffer.

In writing about injurious childhood experiences, Stolorow and Atwood (1992: 54) divide an injury into two parts. In the language of self-psychology, the child experiences an initial self-object failure by the caregiver (anger, lack of attention). This brings a painful emotional response and the child longs for an empathic response from the carer: 'Pain is not pathology. It is the absence of adequate atunement and responsiveness to the child's emotional reactions that renders them unendurable and thus a source of traumatic states and psychopathology'.

In some circumstances the pain caused by the transgression may not be as traumatic as the offender's response when challenged. An empathic response, an apology and some attempt to make reparations helps prevent this secondary injury to the self – an injury caused by being in a world where they cannot have their truth compassionately understood and accepted.

One respondent said that, although he could rarely completely put an injustice behind him, he could go a long way towards this if he could find an excuse for the behaviour in some rational way. This links with other respondents who said that, apart from an apology, it helped to understand the person's motivation for his or her behaviour. Was there a personal element in it? Was it random or thoughtless rather than intentional? This links with Chapter 6, where Masters explores the way mediation is being used in the criminal justice system, offering victims of crime the chance to explore such issues.

The final element mentioned by respondents was commitment. As one wrote, 'I want the other person to make a commitment to try not to do it again'. For her, it was the extent of the effort the person made that was important. Another wrote that what was crucial was not repeating the behaviour, particularly in situations of abuse or negligence. She saw time as being necessary for the person to trust that a real change has taken place.

All this supposes an unjust, one-sided act where the wrongdoer admits guilt and tries to make amends. Wrongs on both sides can make it easier to feel understanding and compassion for the other. There is more potential for recognising the similarities, for making allowances. However, there may be a competitive struggle over whose wound is greater, who is the more culpable. The process of each being able to offer regret, to fully hear the impact this has had on the other, and to let go of blaming the other, may be just as fraught where both carry some of the blame.

Where the wrong is not acknowledged

Where the wrong is not acknowledged, the trauma is intensified. A discussion of why people find it difficult to say sorry and admit guilt is beyond the scope of this chapter. Fear, whether of legal retribution or of condemnation within the community or profession is important. People may be trying to avoid admitting to themselves what they have done. The person who has been harmed is left both with the horror of what has happened and the added horror that their reality is denied. Letting go of bitterness, resentment, the desire for revenge, is harder here. How can you stop being angry when the wrongdoer denies there is anything to be angry about? How do you begin to feel compassion where you are not being offered compassion?

Victims of medical accidents have, until recently, rarely been told the truth. They were left coping both with the injury, or bereavement, not knowing for certain what had caused it. Until recent years, family and friends often found it hard to believe the doctor was to blame. So support was muted or people withdrew from them. Those working with people who were abused in childhood will have heard similar accounts.

In these circumstances what clients have told me they want from a therapist is someone who will believe them. Their first need is for someone who can *really* empathise with what they have been through. This has implications for therapists, not least because they may not know whether the doctor was negligent or whether a person was sexually abused. This is a tension therapists must face, as there seems little doubt that there is a healing in being believed. While empathy is important for the genuineness of the client's belief, may there not come a time when it helps to explore its validity?

Letting go of negative judgement and developing compassion for the wrongdoer

An apology and reparation helps restore a person's self-esteem and contributes to his or her ability to feel empathy towards the wrongdoer. Some people are able, as Baures' (1996) research showed, to let go of their negative judgement and feel compassion even in circumstances of major wrongdoing. One respondent wrote, in the questionnaire, that it is important to recognise any responsibility we may have in what has happened. Another thought that 'the ability to accept our own shadow side and remember the times we have hurt another helps'. A belief in the fallibility of human nature can make it easier in some situations to accept another person's fallibility, including their inability to own up to their wrongdoing. Several found biblical messages of forgiveness an inspiration.

When all else fails, one person wrote of the need to check: 'What do I gain, or lose, from offering compassion and forgiveness?' For another, what gave him the belief in forgiveness was the awareness, in countries such as Ireland and Israel, that violence begets violence and there is value in someone who has suffered saying 'enough, let us stop the cycle here'.

Holding onto negative judgement and withholding compassion

As I wrote earlier, many completing the questionnaire believed it is possible to let go of feelings of bitterness and get on with life without forgiveness. Jeanne Safer (1999) has turned the religious argument on its head by linking morality with unforgiveness. She writes of *moral unforgivers* – people holding onto their negative judgement as a way of making a stand against injustice. Unforgiveness can be in the face of others telling them they are wrong or should put it behind them. The morality in the stand is both in telling the truth and in not colluding with the wrongdoer to appease others. Jane said, 'I can never forgive the doctors for Alan's death. I can only fight to prevent it happening again – I don't know if they think they made a mistake.' This echoes the words of Elie Wiesel when he received the Nobel Peace Prize in 1986: 'There may be times when we are powerless to prevent injustice, but there must never be a time when we fail to protest'.

Safer (1999) writes of one client's struggle to cope with the demands of a mother who seemed to have no insight into the lies she told, the lack of love she offered. Finally, the client wrote to her mother stating that what she had done was wrong. There was no question of forgiveness. However, the client's resentment and panic abated. She was able to begin to let go because of being clear in her moral judgement. In time she began to feel some compassion and had some limited contact based firmly on her assertion that certain behaviours were wrong. The reconciliation was based on her *not forgiving*.

Safer also writes of *reformed unforgivers*. Here the person has spent perhaps years accepting and excusing unacceptable behaviour. As Safer puts it, forgiveness becomes confused with submerging normal reactions to mistreatment. She gives an example of a 75-year-old who finally realised she did not have to keep on forgiving and severed contact with someone who had been endlessly critical of her. She described the relief of letting go of the relationship.

Giving up the hope of a better past

Stroebe and Schut (in Thompson 2002) caution against the notion of stages of loss. They write in terms of two 'orientations': the loss orientation and the restoration orientation. The notions of 'fully facing' the loss and 'moving on' must be, therefore, treated with caution. They suggest the person who has had to face a loss or trauma will long continue to oscillate between the loss and rebuilding his or her future life. As one respondent wrote, 'We have a good relationship now and I feel stronger. I have long got over his affair, but I know, deep down, I've marked his card. He'll never do that to me again'.

To be moving on, the person needs to have felt sufficiently powerful both to face the pain and the future. As Jampolsky strikingly puts it, it involves giving up the hope of a better past (1985). Kepner writes of the survivor's needs to 'reorientate' to what has happened as being past, only 'an aspect, not the whole of her nature' (1999: 144). To do this, she has to have some way of making sense, of becoming at peace with her life experiences and history. In these terms, the survivor becomes more than the loss, more than the anger, more than the search for justice. As one client said of her child who had died, 'She is part of me, wherever I go. And I also have a new life'.

Ending comments

What is clear from the research is that, for some, 'letting go' can be another phrase for forgiving the other person. It can also have quite a distinct meaning, involving distancing from the damaging bitterness and hurt caused by the actions of another. The ability to let go of bitterness may stem from forgiveness. It may equally well stem from the clarity of our decision to hold another responsible and in the wrong.

Like Safer (1999), I believe the reality, for most of us, is that there is a continuum between forgiveness and unforgiveness, between letting go and bitterness, between the desire for revenge and love. What is important is the need to check whether compassion equals compliance, whether moral love equals self-righteousness. This last sentence betrays my continued concern about forgiveness, yet I have a strong belief in the value of human relationships and the need to transcend wrongdoing if we are to avoid tragic cycles of retaliation and revenge. As the Chinese proverb states: 'Whoever opts for revenge should dig two graves'. Healthy relationships and our own health depend on our capacity to find peace with our past in whatever way is appropriate to us. I will end with the words, which I have slightly modified, sent to me by one of the respondents to my questionnaire: 'I will tame my memories so that they become my companions, *as* I choose'. For me, I'll stick to the ambiguity of *letting go*.

References

Baures, M. (1996) Letting go of bitterness and hate, *Journal of Humanistic Psychology*, 36(1): 75–90.

Berne, E. (1972) *What Do You Say After You Say Hello?* London: Corgi.

Davis, L. (1990) *The Courage to Heal Workbook*. London: HarperCollins.

DiBlasio, F.A. (1993) The role of social workers' religious beliefs in helping family members forgive, *Families in Society*, 74: 163–70.

DiBlasio, F.A. and Proctor, J.H. (1993) Therapists and the clinical use of forgiveness, *American Journal of Family Therapy*, 21: 175–84.

Dobbins, R.D. (2000) Psychotherapy with Pentecostal Protestants, in P.S. Richards and A.E. Bergin (eds) *Handbook of Pychotherapy and Religious Diversity*. Washington: American Psychological Association.

Enright, R., Freedman, S. and Rique, J. (1998) The psychology of interpersonal forgiveness, in R.D. Enright and J. North (eds) *Exploring Forgiveness*. Madison, WI: University of Wisconsin Press.

Holloway, R. (2002) *On Forgiveness*. Edinburgh: Canongate Books.

Jampolsky, G. (1985) *Goodbye to Guilt: Releasing Fear through Forgiveness*. New York: Bantam Books.

Kepner, J.I. (1999) *Healing Tasks*. San Francisco: Jossey-Bass.

Lampen, J. (1994) *Mending Hurts*, 2nd edn. London: Quaker Home Service.

Neimeyer, R.A. and Anderson, A. (2002) Meaning reconstruction theory, in N. Thompson (ed.) *Loss and Grief*. Basingstoke, Hampshire: Palgrave.

Safer, J. (1999) Must you forgive?, *Psychology Today*, July/August.

Steiner, J. (1993) *Psychic Retreats: Pathological Organisations of the Personality in Psychotic, Neurotic and Borderline Patients*. London: Routledge.

Stolorow, D.G. and Atwood, G.E. (1992) *Contexts of Being*. Hillsdale, NJ: Analytic Press.

Thompson, N. (2002) *Loss and Grief*. Basingstoke, Hampshire: Palgrave.

Thurston, N.S. (2000) Psychotherapy with evangelical and fundamentalist Christians, in P.S. Richards and A.E. Bergin (eds) *Handbook of Pychotherapy and Religious Diversity*. Washington: American Psychological Association.

Weldon, F. (1975) *Female Friends*. London: Penguin.

Yalom, I.D. (1980) *Existential Psychotherapy*. New York: Basic Books.

Chapter 4

The role of forgiveness in working with couples

Jane Cooper and Maria Gilbert

Introduction

In this chapter we look at forgiveness in the context of couples work, and suggest a model that can be used both to work from and monitor progress. Forgiveness in couples work is somewhat different to working with a single client. The perpetrator of a perceived injustice is present in the room together with the victim, and emotions run high. It is important to remember that it is a client's right to choose whether or not to forgive and that the person must not be under duress to do so. The therapist needs to hold a meta-perspective on the relationship for both parties, while recognising deeply felt emotions on both sides. There is a difference between forgiveness and reconciliation in the sense of agreeing to stay together and progress the relationship. A couple may choose to reconcile but not forgive, or the act of forgiveness may only happen after a considerable length of time, maybe after due reparation has been made. True forgiveness is an active process, and can only happen when the depth of hurt or injustice and life changing aspects have been fully experienced by both partners in the relationship. This process of forgiveness involves the whole person, and in transactional analysis terms needs to involve all three ego states: parent, adult and child.

The quality of forgiveness in couples work

The question of forgiveness is an important feature of couples work, especially where partners have developed deep-seated resentments about the behaviour of the other, often stretching over many years of the relationship. We see forgiveness as a two-way process involving both the transgressor and the person transgressed against; an interactive process involving both parties.

Berne (1961) developed the concept of ego states for understanding the human personality. He saw each of us as having a parent ego state (made up of the introjected 'others' from our childhood), an adult ego state (that part of us that is in touch with current reality) and a child ego state (the memories we have laid down of our own childhood history). At any given moment we will be operating from one of these ego states. Forgiveness is multi-layered and sometimes a person may 'forgive' someone from the adult ego state but not from the 'hurt child' or the 'angry parent' ego states (Berne 1961). For example, understanding her husband's appallingly abusive childhood allowed a battered wife to forgive her husband at the adult level when she appreciated his history and understood the nature of his retaliatory behaviour, but at a deeper level in her child state she could not forgive him for hurting her and her children, nor in terms of her value system could she condone his violent behaviour in the family. Her adult understanding of the childhood causes that predisposed him towards violent behaviour led her to see him in a more compassionate light. She was, however, still left with the hurt on behalf of herself and her children and with the knowledge that he did, as an adult, have a choice in the matter. Although more compassionate towards him, she could not see him as exempt from blame, nor could she accept his protestations that he 'couldn't help it' as the behaviour 'simply comes over me'. For those couples therapists working from a transactional analysis perspective therefore, forgiveness does need to involve acceptance and letting go from all three ego states. The person forgiving needs to feel compassion and understanding from the adult state, a warmth, energy and openness from the child to reach out again to the other, and parental agreement that values are not still being transgressed, overlooked or minimised. This process, to be successful in repairing a relationship, requires some careful contracting involving agreements to behave differently in the future. The couples' therapist needs to monitor carefully that these contracts involve the full participation of both partners.

We consider forgiveness an intersubjective process involving the full participation of both partners in a couple. The trangressor needs to experience sadness and remorse, accounting fully for the transgression, and the person transgressed against needs to be open to these feelings, to forgive and let go of resentments. Forgiveness can only truly happen when the transgressor asks for forgiveness, knowing the full extent of what the effect on the other has been and accounting for the impact of his or her behaviour on that other or others. Saying a simple 'sorry' is often not enough, and forgiveness when none has been asked for frequently does not work effectively for either person. The Christian message of forgiveness, although attractive in principle, seems to leave loose ends in the relationship – for example, if the transgressor has not requested forgiveness or shows no move towards remorse or reparation. This is an important step in the process; forgiveness must be actively sought and welcomed by both partners.

A good example of this is a couple who survived an affair by the man early in their marriage. The wife was able from an outside perspective to see how very hard it was for him to confess to her, to have put himself in a shame-filled place and to admit to what he had done, realising too that this is what his father had done to his mother. The man's willingness to talk about his shame and guilt and his wife's openness to his risk led to a fuller life for both of them. The marriage grew in strength and survives now, 30 years on, without resentment having festered in that period. Truth and reconciliation, as the Truth and Reconciliation Commission (TRC) in South Africa demonstrated, can sometimes assist people to forgive and come to terms with deeply painful experiences. This requires of people the willingness to reflect on their previous behaviour with honesty and courage so that both parties are able to understand, forgive and achieve some form of reconciliation with the aim of moving on from the painful past and building a new and better future together.

We have found that where the trangressor is prepared to offer some form of reparation in this process of seeking forgiveness, full reconciliation can be achieved. Reparation involves making amends in a manner that can be understood and received by the hurt party. It seems very human that if we have been hurt, some reparative act will seem 'justifiable' and appropriate. Justice will not only be seen to be done but will also be felt to have taken place! Acts of reparation need to be agreed as appropriate by both partners as 'fitting the crime' so that there can be a sense of justice experienced on both sides. Reparation facilitates the final letting go of resentment and paves the way for reconciliation and a different quality of relationship. We find that forgiveness and reparation work well when they are linked to new contracts and agreements for the future, aimed at averting similar events from recurring. The concept of the contract is described well in transactional analysis (TA) and involves a mutual agreement about reaching specifically stated goal(s) with which both partners can identify (Sills 1997). The therapist needs to ensure that these contracts are realistic and address the basis of both partners' concerns in order to be really effective in the process of reconciliation and healing. For example, if there has been a breakdown in communication in a relationship the contract may involve one partner contracting not to use bullying tactics to get his or her way in the process of trying to resolve differences, while the other party agrees not to withdraw and avoid important issues between them by running away from confrontation.

Where only one person is involved in 'forgiving' another, such as a partner dealing with abandonment by the other, we prefer to think of this rather as a process of 'letting go' rather than one of forgiveness. Such one-sided letting go is often important where the other is either no longer invested in the relationship or may no longer be around. We would, however, not class this as forgiveness in the way we conceive of this process (which needs to be mutual and interactive). But such a process of letting go may be vital to enable someone to move on from a past relationship in which they have become stuck.

A full understanding of each other's feelings regarding the event or events that are the subject of forgiveness is crucially important to full closure. For example, a couple came complaining of the wife's loss of interest in sex, since the birth of their third child 18 months before. The husband had been in a yacht race when his wife went into labour and arrived back just in time for the normal delivery. He could not comprehend her anger at him, which had lasted the full 18 months. He had apologised many times but was not really sure what he had done to offend her. This delivery had been the easiest of all three, both mother and child had come home early from hospital, he had taken time off to be with them, so why was she still so angry with him that she would not allow sex? In the couples therapy, the therapist supported her to relive that episode, recalling how frightened she had been at being in a strange country, vulnerable, with two small children to care for and her baby due any time. Her anger was that he had even considered doing the race when she was in such a vulnerable position, especially when he could so easily have got out of it. He had not before this understood or appreciated her fear and vulnerability prior to the delivery and was subsequently able to apologise to her for this omission in full understanding of the experience for her. This done, they resumed their sexual relationship. This capacity to enter into and appreciate the significance of the experience of the other is the basis for effective and full forgiveness which then allows the couple to move on from the stuck place in their relationship.

Not all events requiring forgiveness are one-sided. Often both partners have contributed to what has gone wrong between them, and then forgiveness may need to come from both sides. In fact, much of our work involves relationships where couples have mutually hurt and offended one another so the process of forgiveness needs to be addressed from both sides. In fact, resentments may have accumulated on both sides over the years in response to many hurts and transgressions which have piled up, and create a barrier between the two people. Until these resentments have been aired, fully acknowledged by both parties and the feelings associated with them given expression, they may continue to fester underneath, poisoning the relationship over a period of years, sometimes over the entire life of the marriage.

Olive and Peter had been married for 50 years and came in crisis. Should they divorce? How could they live apart? What were the implications in relation to their family and social connections if they did? They were very unhappy with each other and it had all come to a head. In therapy they dragged up every little resentment they felt towards the other from the day they first met. None of this had ever been aired or let go of and it was important for the therapist to facilitate this sharing process so that both of them felt heard by the other. Because of the many resentments and hurts harboured by both of them, therapy it seemed would be slow and arduous, exploring each resentment and trying to encourage each partner to see the other's perspective. However, one of the advantages of working with a couple rather than an individual came into play here, since once they had started the process of acknowledging and expressing their resentments, they were able to continue doing this between sessions and soon came to a point were they could let go of the past and move on to a new way of being together.

A relational basis for forgiveness

Forgiveness calls for a particular form of maturity; for the capacity to empathise with and enter into the experience of the other person.

In order to achieve full forgiveness, the person 'forgiving' will, in our view, need to practise 'inclusion', defined by Buber ([1923] 1996) as the capacity to be grounded in one's own experience and at the same time to enter into the world of the other. It is important in this process of inclusion to hold both one's own and the other's perspective, while appreciating the interaction between these. In this way the person can begin to see how it is possible that the contentious event(s) took place and what both parties may have contributed to the misunderstanding. The process of inclusion implies the capacity to maintain a meta-perspective on the relationship so that a person is able to appreciate the impact of his or her behaviour on the other and assess the other's response to them in terms of the interactive process. This means in effect developing an ability to remain grounded in one's own experience and refining the capacity for entering empathically into the world of the other without losing a sense of one's self. At the same time it requires the capacity to be able to move to a meta-view of the relationship and see it as it were from the outside as a spectator might do. This is not something any person can maintain for any length of time but a meta-view from both within and without seems crucial for a real appreciation of the impact of our behaviour on others. We see this as the basis for long-lasting forgiveness.

The process of inclusion depends on the person developing a sense of 'object constancy' and whole object relatedness in the process of their early development. 'Object constancy' involves a capacity to retain our sense of the other even when that person is not present and to maintain a sense of connectedness with the other over time as the 'same' person. In the process of growing up with ordinary, good enough parents, children gradually develop the capacity to see their parents as 'whole' people, neither good nor bad, but having a balance of qualities. In the process of coming to terms with what we do and do not like in our parents we gradually develop an integrated image of them that includes their strengths and weaknesses, their 'good' and 'bad' parts. This is called whole object relatedness, in object relations theory, when I no longer experience just a 'part' of the other in my experience of them, but I begin to appreciate the whole person, 'warts and all'! It is this developed ability that underlies the capacity for full forgiveness: 'One must be able to hold two emotionally contradictory images in mind, one of the object as frustrating or harmful and one of the object as valuable and loved. It is then that forgiveness is possible'

(Hamilton 1988: 109). In this process the child also develops a balanced sense of self, bringing the good and bad aspects of self together into an integrated self-image. The result of this process of developing object constancy means that 'we can see ourselves as essentially good, but we also acknowledge some less desirable qualities' (Hamilton 1988: 107). If a person has developed object constancy in this way, then that person will be able to acknowledge their faults and 'own up to them' in a relationship; nor will they experience such 'owning up' as undermining their self-worth completely or destroying their self-image. They will be able to accept realistically that their behaviour has impacted negatively on another and has harmed that person, and be open to ask for forgiveness and make reparation.

For people who grow up in more stressful and destructive circumstances than those who are fortunate enough to experience 'an average expectable environment' (Hartmann 1939), this capacity for whole object relations may not develop; instead they may survive by a process of splitting off the 'good' from the 'bad' experiences. So in effect they may not develop whole object relatedness but rather 'split' object relatedness. Such a person will experience the self and other as either all good or all bad. For them the process of forgiveness may be difficult, either because they cannot move from the view of the other as wholly bad and unforgivable if they are the injured party, or because they expect to be seen immediately as 'good' and acceptable again because they feel sorry and have said so! Either way, there will be a lack of completion in the process because not all the other's experience (or their own) is being accounted for by this process of minimisation. Such a person will have difficulty in accepting any redeeming qualities in the other when they are angry and feeling vengeful; similarly when they require forgiveness they will expect this to come automatically because they feel sorry and this leads them to feel good about themselves. In neither of these processes will the actual experience or feelings of the other be taken into account except minimally, as they suit the person's frame of reference. This process of discounting or minimising the impact of behaviour does not bode well for a full process of forgiveness. This is a sobering thought because it may well be that forgiveness is out of the reach of certain people until they are able to repair their fractured early object relationships and appreciate the fullness of others in their many facets. In such cases, couples work may not be the intervention of first choice: some other therapeutic intervention may serve the individuals better.

Zoe and Kevin came at Zoe's instigation when she perceived the couple as having a problem in their relationship. Zoe felt unable to enjoy the experience of climax when they had sex. During the therapy sessions Kevin delighted in ridiculing and persecuting Zoe, and openly invited the therapist to do so too. When this was pointed out to him he saw clearly what he was doing but could not find any other way of relating to her. Joint therapy was discontinued and they were advised to seek individual help. He refused, saying there was nothing wrong with him. She did pursue individual therapy and after a short while she left him. Forgiveness therapy was not appropriate for these clients.

Enright and Fitzgibbons (2000) suggest a process model of forgiveness therapy, which we have used and adapted into our framework. There are four stages in the process and these are slightly different for each of the parties. Each stage may be arrived at simultaneously by the partners or at differing times. However, it may happen that partners do not move through all these stages and become stuck at certain points. Sometimes this requires going back and recycling some of the stages again. The stages are shown in Figure 4.1.

Each stage contains several factors that need to be explored. In work with couples, that means feelings can be looked at on both

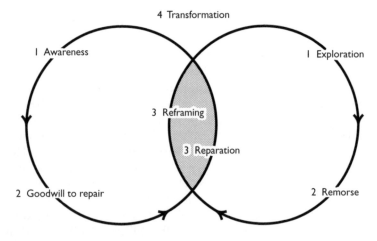

Figure 4.1   Process model of forgiveness

sides of the dispute at once. This also requires the therapist to be vigilant in the work, allowing and deepening awareness of feelings while somehow remaining neutral in the relationship. The good thing about working with a couple however, is that the work will be continuing between sessions, and major shifts or reframing may take place outside the therapy room. This may be the result of an informal process or may also be related to specific 'homework' assignments.

Stage 1: awareness/exploration

In this stage a full exploration of those feelings associated with the transgression needs to be facilitated by the therapist. This may take time as the partners may first need to overcome their resistance to sharing feelings that are associated with shame and embarrassment. Those who choose not to forgive may only go as far as this part of the process, since, having identified the feelings they may decide that for them this is an 'unforgivable' offence. We respect that for some people the hurt may be so deep that any question of forgiving the other person may simply not be their choice. Therapy may need to look at the process of letting go instead.

At this stage, the therapist needs to enquire about the following.

What really happened?

What are the concrete facts? This exploration helps to deepen awareness and gain insight into the nature of the offence and its effects on both people. Is the offended party's anger real or misplaced? Is there denial or repression of anger? There may be more than one incident to forgive – if so, the therapist advises a start with the most recent. It is important for the therapist to elicit the facts in detail from both parties so that they both experience being heard by the therapist and by the other partner.

Susan and Edward married after a long and exciting courtship, then came a complete cessation of sex. Eliciting the facts in therapy it appeared that Susan was really looking forward to sex on their wedding night. It would be something special she said. Edward did not know this was how she felt and was exhausted by the day's festivities, so went to sleep. She was furious with him and refused to have sex subsequently but never told him why. By talking about what happened (or rather what did not happen), in detail, he was able to see and appreciate her disappointment and hurt. He was then able to surprise her by secretly transforming their bedroom into a replica of a Bedouin tent and gave her the wedding night she desired!

As the injured party gains awareness he or she may experience anger or become even more angry than before

This needs to be acknowledged and allowed full expression. In a couple situation it is important to recognise that it is the behaviour of the offender and not the person of the offender that has caused the hurt. The therapist can aid in this process by encouraging the couple to talk to each other in terms of, 'when you said or did this I felt angry' rather than 'you make me angry' or 'you never take me into account'. This encouragement to own feelings and to mention specific offending behaviours leaves the way open for change. The offended party is then given a choice either to relinquish the behaviour that causes the distress to the other or to continue in the knowledge they are causing pain. In such a case, is there underlying anger and resentment contributing on their part, which needs to be explored? The expression of anger in the therapy room needs to be tempered with the avoidance of persecution of the other. It may be helpful to use a cushion to represent the offender and allow the injured party to vent their feelings there. In this way their anger may be heard by the offender, who is not using their energy in defending themselves from attack. Similarly to get the injured party to tell the therapist how they feel with the other listening can serve as well. This is aimed to assist both partners to develop a meta-perspective on the process in the relationship so that each becomes more aware of their own impact on the other.

Is there shame or embarrassment?

Shame can be a particularly hurtful part of the experience. How the person feels viewed by the wider community can be an important factor. For the perpetrator, is there shame heaped on them in their community or culture? For the victim, is this person seen to have colluded in the victimisation? There may also be shame at not having recognised a problem, or feeling you deserved the offence committed against you in the first place (as in cases of domestic violence). Such judgements can only add to the pain already experienced.

A man from a deeply religious background left his wife for another woman. He was then ostracised by his community and family. He then had to deal with his own betrayal of deeply-held personal beliefs combined with a complete loss of social support and humiliation from those he loved and respected.

Effects on everyday life

The therapist needs to assist partners to acknowledge the emotional energy invested by both of them in dealing with the offence. In addition the therapist may need to address the type of obsessional thinking, or preoccupation with the event that people may use to hold onto the past in an unproductive manner. The clients may dream about the incident and a large part of their life may be interfered with because of their constant ruminations. This debilitating process needs to be acknowledged as it may completely undermine their efforts to achieve any resolution.

Ginny came with her partner Jane of 25 years, unable to forgive her for a single brief affair she had a year previously while Ginny was away nursing a sick relative. The therapy session explored the amount of personal energy Ginny was expending, thinking, fantasising and dreaming about this affair. Probably most of her waking life and some of her sleep was taken up by the offence, a year on. The therapist assisted her in the process of letting go of these ruminations and focusing on moving forward in the relationship by addressing the fears that were underlying the process.

Comparison

This can take different forms and be done internally or expressed openly to the other. This process may involve a direct comparison of the one person's behaviour with that of the other – for example: 'You were off enjoying yourself while I was giving birth to our child'. It can also involve a comparison with a third party as in the case of an affair: 'He is better looking than me, more sexually experienced, and so on'. Such comparisons can be used to fuel fights and are best addressed directly in the couples sessions.

Geeta was consumed by comparing herself with the person with whom her partner had an affair. She thought constantly about how she looked in comparison to the other woman. Was the other prettier, was she sexier? How could she, Geeta, live up to this fantasised perfection? She lost confidence in her appearance and her libido diminished to nothing. The therapist focused on this undermining process and helped her to articulate the uncertainties she was currently experiencing in her relationship, as well as helping her to reach out for emotional contact with her partner.

Loss of fantasy

There is a need to recognise that the relationship faces inextricable permanent change. Things will never be like they were before. People carry a picture or image of their relationship in their minds. This may be based partly in reality and partly in fantasy and may also reside in the unconscious hope of finding the idealised 'other'. The view or image of the relationship carried in the minds of each partner will have been fractured and will inevitably need to change in response to the events being discussed. Such a loss of the idealised image of the relationship will need to be tackled directly by both people. This will result in a more realistic (hopefully) and workable relationship image. This may also result in a change in perception in the basic philosophy of how the world works. In couples work this may mean the loss of fantasies about how relationships work, challenging the partners' internal scripts, cultural and religious expectations.

Stage 2: goodwill to repair/remorse

In this phase the couple develop deeper insights that may lead to ideas of remorse on the offender's part and goodwill to repair on the part of the injured. They may, through the increased awareness of the emotions in stage 1, move away from a quest for revenge and experience a change of heart. They may then move on in their relationship where they may be willing to consider forgiveness as an option. It is important here to make sure they understand what forgiveness really is, and what it is not:

- forgiveness is abandonment of resentment (to which they have a right) and adopting a friendlier attitude (to which the offender may not have a right);

- there is a distinction between forgiveness and condoning, excusing, forgetting or reconciling;
- forgiving does not make the forgiver weak in any way, and does not give the offending party licence to offend again.

They may then commit to forgive. The therapist asks for a commitment not to condemn the other or take subtle revenge. With a couple this may mean behaving in a civilised manner towards the other, even when angry or upset. This process may need to involve a focus on conflict resolution and the discussion of very specific steps that both partners agree to in the process of 'fighting fair'. These agreements give each party some control over what has happened and how they will respond in the future. They have some choices as to how they behave. This may be firmed up in contracts that outline specific behaviours to be honoured on both sides. To start Mike and Peter on the path to forgiveness they were asked by the therapist independently to be civil to the other, irrespective of how the other behaved. After a short while both reported a lessening of animosity and a more peaceful atmosphere between them.

Stage 3: reframing/reparation

This stage is where the couple can co-create a 'penance' to end the punishment, and the therapist can encourage this by looking at the following.

Reframing

Here the therapist encourages the couple to look deeper into the other, to put themselves in the other's shoes, to explore whether the offended party contributed towards the offensive behaviour. Is there a need for reparation on both sides? Can the couple co-create it? What was the relationship like before? Can they use any of that to help them move on now? Is their cosmic/spiritual perspective useful in recognising the inherent worth of the other?

Carl had a brief affair after the birth of Beatrice's first baby. In the sessions we explored what it was like for him to feel jealous of the attention his partner was paying to her newborn. He felt he had lost his place with her. He was resentful and petulant, and what was worse she did not notice. On hearing his sense of feeling lost and abandoned, Beatrice was able to see for herself what had contributed to driving him away. She was then able to take responsibility for her part in the process, and chose to make time for him as well as the baby. He in turn, feeling more secure, was able to take more of an active role in the care of their child, which freed her up to spend more time with him. In this case the therapist enabled the partners to gain a deeper understanding of one another's experience.

Showing empathy and compassion

Empathy is morally neutral; it involves a non-judgemental acceptance of the other, recognising that it is the act that is condemned not the person. Compassion is a moral emotion whose goal is the other's good; it demonstrates the capacity to take a stance of forgiveness towards the other. By displaying empathy and compassion, partners begin to appreciate the essential differences between them and their experience of the world so that they no longer assume that the other must experience things exactly the same way they do!

Beatrice showed empathy towards Carl, realising that although his having an affair was not to be condoned, he was with her in therapy and trying to make amends. She went on to show compassion when she chose to react to her awareness positively and make more time for him. She also realised there was a difference between them. Her delight in being with and caring for the new baby, to the exclusion of all else, was not seen by him in the same light. The therapist's task was to ensure that the partners listened carefully to one another and took time to understand the other's experience.

Bearing the pain

As the couple mature emotionally they can begin to accept what has happened from an adult ego perspective. Recognising the scar but no longer feeling the pain, requires courage, and they may well realise at this stage that they are stronger than they thought. This can deepen their relationship, as they move from the status of victims to survivors.

Julie and Mark had spent several years unable to have sexual intercourse because of Mark's total impotence. They had tried many different therapies and medical treatments to achieve penetration, but all in vain. In therapy the pain and grief over the loss of their sex life came to the surface and they both sobbed. The therapist facilitated the expression of the grief. By the next session they were a changed couple. In being supported by the therapist to acknowledge their pain they realised how strong their relationship was and how their experience had forged them into what they were now. In their maturation they had grown in their love and trust for each other, and were able to let go of the past and discover new ways of being intimate with each other.

Offering an olive branch

A smile, an expression of concern, or a diminution of resentment may all serve as an olive branch to the other. Such signs will prepare the way for a movement into the final stage.

Nico and Neo had argued for many years. Neo had persuaded Nico to move from his native country where he had friends and family to support him, to an isolated village where the residents kept to themselves. Nico had been unable to forgive Neo for years and behaved towards him in a sullen and resentful way. Nico was asked by the therapist to experiment with saying something appreciative about Neo in the therapy room. A long pause ensued before Nico finally said, 'He's got lovely blue eyes'. Both of them broke into smiles and held hands. This olive branch certainly helped!

Stage 4: transformation

Find meaning

At this stage couples need to find a rational reason or an affirmative way of thinking that makes sense of the suffering. As in all traumatic experiences, trauma in marriage will radically challenge the partners' frames of reference and the meaning that they give to life. Did they have to go through this in order to strengthen the relationship? Does this new narrative make sense in the light of forgiveness and reparation? The couple will jointly construct a way of viewing their experience that leads to a new and enriched perspective on their relationship.

One couple's honesty in sharing about their respective extra-marital affairs, and their subsequent choice to stop and be exclusively with each other, changed their view of marriage. It was no longer a place to act out their resentments but a partnership to be valued and shared. They said perhaps they had to go through all this pain as a 'test', in order to reach this sense of contentment.

Becoming aware of affective transformation

With humanity and humility the couple will move into a process of affective transformation. This can lead to a deepening love between them, love being the rational application of goodwill to the other. At this stage the couple can celebrate their journey through the process of forgiveness to reconciliation and renewal.

In the exploration of the process of forgiveness in the therapeutic context another couple learned just how much they valued and loved each other. Mutual respect had grown, and they started actively to support the other in their individual lives and careers. They wanted to mark their new way of being together and decided to renew their marriage vows. Rather different from the 'shotgun' wedding that had taken place 15 years before!

When forgiveness is not possible

In our experience we have found that there are occasions on which forgiveness is simply not possible. Each person appears to have a limit, a point beyond which he or she experiences certain actions as 'unforgivable'. When someone has passed that point the person feels pushed too far and beyond a stage where forgiveness seems possible.

This process is often the result of being on the receiving end of repeated transgressions in relation to which the aggressor appears to have experienced no remorse (or only muttered superficial apologies), so that the person who has been hurt moves beyond a stage where forgiveness is an option. The injured party has usually become worn down by years of suffering and aborted attempts to initiate a constructive dialogue. In such a case we would respect the person's freedom of choice and not put pressure on them to 'forgive and forget'. This stage may also be characterised by the person feeling indifferent, beyond any feelings for the other any more, as if they have been drained of any affect and responsiveness. A person who had repeatedly tried to get through to her partner over many years without success, when he finally appeared ready to request forgiveness and make reparation, expressed her position this way: 'I am afraid that too much water has passed under the bridges that were waiting to be built!' Her sentiment was poignant and indicated years of ceaseless and fruitless effort to reach the other person.

Conclusion

Our work with couples in the area of forgiveness has supported our belief in the capacity of human beings to address their pain, face the implications of their actions and move on to transformation in their partnerships. We are available to people for this process which we regard as a mutual and intersubjective event which requires the full participation of both partners. In some cases people may be so caught up in bearing grudges that they have very little energy or interest left for rebuilding the relationship. We acknowledge that these people may be unwilling to re-engage with one another in what is bound to be both a challenging and soul-searching process. We would never impose the process of forgiveness outlined above on people unless they are both open and willing to participate. One-sided 'forgiveness' is not in our view true forgiveness!

References

Berne, E. (1961) *Transactional Analysis in Psychotherapy*. New York: Ballantine Books.

Buber, M. ([1923] 1996) *I and Thou*, trans. W. Kaufman. New York: Touchstone.

Enright, R.D. and Fitzgibbons, R.P. (2000) *Helping Clients Forgive: An Empirical Guide for Resolving Anger and Restoring Hope*. Washington: American Psychological Association.

Hamilton, G.H. (1988) *Self and Others: Object Relations Theory in Practice*. Northvale, NJ: Jason Aronson.

Hartmann, H. (1939) *Ego Psychology and the Problem of Adaptations*. New York: International Universities Press.

Sills, C. (ed.) (1997) *Contracts in Counselling*. London: Sage.

Chapter 5

Organisations and forgiveness: the challenge

Michael Carroll

Introduction

This chapter only makes sense when a certain perspective on 'organisations' is accepted, and in keeping with the title of the chapter, this could be the biggest challenge of all. Seeing organisations (be they private, public, voluntary, educational, industrial, religious or medical) as machines or objects automatically excludes having a chapter in this book entitled 'organisations and forgiveness'. Machines or objects cannot forgive nor is it credible for individuals to forgive machines even though, technically, we can be disappointed in our washing machine or car or house. Forgiveness includes the context of choice, being able to intentionally hurt and to choose to give the gift of letting go, and redirect energies away from grudges. Where there is no choice, or ability to choose, there is no forgiveness. Only humans can forgive and be forgiven.

From this springboard (seeing organisations as living communities), this chapter will look at how a variety of people (consultants, psychologists, mediators and counsellors) who work with different organisations, and with individuals within organisations, can utilise 'forgiveness', when appropriate, as one possible intervention among others.

Organisations: machines or living communities?

Once we begin to think of organisations as living organisms, as communities of people who have a life and being other than being solely a collection of individuals, we can then consider the possibility that they can forgive and be forgiven. However, this is a difficult transitional mindset to make. Most of our ways of thinking centre on the concept of organisations as machines or objects. De Geus makes the point well: 'What if we thought about a company as a living being?' (1997: 2), and goes on to show how the machine concept permeates our thinking about organisations. Companies and organisations are owned (like machines), exist for reasons conceived of by their builders (like machines who have no say in their destiny), with purposes, like making money for their owners, if they are private (like machines), are controlled by their operators (like machines), are fixed, static (like machines), can only change if someone changes them (like machines), have only the sense of identity given them by their builders (like machines), do not have their own purposes and capacity for autonomy (like machines), will run down unless they are maintained (like machines), have members who are 'human resources' waiting to be used (like machines) and cannot learn (like machines).

Thinking of the organisation as a living being, however, reverses all these features – how horrible to think of an organisation (a living being) being owned by someone. Most of us have long since moved from the idea of one person owning another. Living beings have their own purposes (over and above the ideas of those who created them), are not controllable by others, create themselves and their reasons for existing, develop and change as they choose, become autonomous and independent and create human communities. Organisations as living entities, as beings, as organisms, are able to learn ('the learning organisation') by themselves rather than being the sum total of the learning of individuals within them. Organisational culture could be defined as what an organisation, as an organisation, has learned.

We have a right to ask organisations – not just the managing director or the shareholders or the board of trustees – to apologise when they have perpetrated actions that have hurt their employees, others or the environment. Like all living beings, organisations need to be sensitive to their environment and their people, have a sense of their identity and who they are, and exist, as De Geus (1997) argues so well, not to make profits or to produce services but to maximise their potential and become the best they can be (like all humans). Not that these two should be exclusive of one another – maximising potential will, hopefully, result in better profits or better services. Often, organisations get the chronology wrong and see products (whether profits or services) as the prime purpose rather than managing talent and potential. From my experience, focusing on the former usually results in creating 'machine companies' and rarely leads to maximising potential, while emphasising the latter often concludes with higher profits and better services.

The organisation as system

Allied to the concept of the organisation as a living being is the notion of the organisation as a system. Briefly, this means that all parts of the organisation are related and connected to other parts and changes in one part herald changes in another. Systems have been described as 'the mutually sustaining interdependent causal relationships amongst . . . the "spheres"' (Smith and Yanowitz 1999: 533). There are connections when we cannot even see connections. Organisations are learning systems (or suffer from learning disabilities) and are as much emotional arenas as they are rational environments (Hinshelwood 2001). Thinking systemically means thinking of the organisation as a totality (and in this case a living system not a dead one) – what are the underlying norms that influence behaviour, what are the unconscious elements that often dehumanise individuals and what are the underlying myths that need to be tackled if the organisation is to change as an organisation? In respect of forgiveness, how can we build into the organisational system a sense of apology, forgiveness and reconciliation when needed?

The psychological contract

A third concept that provides a backcloth to 'organisations and forgiveness' is the idea of the psychological contract. This concept makes some sense of why imagined hurts are as real and painful to individuals as are real (objective) hurts. While there will be a contract of work (overt) outlining agreements, job descriptions etc., there will also be a 'psychological contract' (covert) which is much more difficult to understand because much of it will be unsaid and unspoken. The psychological contract will be 'head agreements' between employees and their organisation (and between the organisation and employees) which include all their expectations, projections and assumptions in respect of their needs and requirements including such elements as:

- The company will give me a job for life
- I will get promotion soon
- If I work hard I will get a pay rise
- If I am nice to people, they will be nice to me
- If I . . . then, others (team, individuals, organisation) will . . .

Many of the facets of psychological contracts are unreasonable, some are perfectly reasonable. But what all elements in the psychological contract have in common is that, by and large, they are not discussed or negotiated with the organisation or the other person in the relationship. The psychological contract is defined as 'an unwritten set of expectations operating at all times between every member of an organisation and the other people in the organisation' (Makin *et al.* 1996: 4). It is the word 'expectations' that distinguishes the psychological contract from other forms of contract.

It is often as a result of the psychological contract being broken that individuals in organisational settings get hurt, disappointed and wounded. To the amazement of the organisation, and others (who know nothing of this 'contract in the head'), an individual accuses them of being unfair, unjust, mean or whatever. A grudge is held that in the view of the organisation is of the individual's own making. From the employee's perspective, an important protocol or tacit agreement has been seriously ruptured.

An example of this is a secretary who had worked out in her head, but not with anyone else, that if she worked through her lunch break she could come in 45 minutes late in the morning. Her manager hated conflict and the situation was not tackled until a new manager was appointed about a year after the secretary had made the decision above. When the new manager confronted the situation all hell broke loose with the secretary taking out a harassment claim against her new manager. More subtle forms of how the psychological contract pertains can be seen where managers collude with employees to change procedures (again without involving anyone else) or where managers impose their own expectations and demands on employees without negotiation or discussion.

Using these three viewpoints (the organisation as living being, the organisation as a system and the psychological contract) this chapter will look at how organisations can forgive and be forgiven. While there are many ways in which this process of two-way forgiveness can take place (e.g. apology, reconciliation, conflict management, team development, policies and procedures, organisational and systems change), the roles of counsellors and consultants who work with organisations and individuals in organisations will be the focus. My own perspective is that forgiveness has to be worked towards, rather than started with, and that it is a process involving a number of stages rather than simply an external procedure to be followed.

Organisations and hurts

Organisations hurt individuals and individuals injure organisations. There are numerous ways in which organisations hurt people. One instance is where individuals feel hurt, disappointed, let down and hold a grudge against another individual where they are both employees of the same organisation. While examples of this kind of hurt could be viewed simply as individual relationship problems, the very fact that they take place within an organisation (company, firm, institution) often makes it an organisational problem (i.e. employers are responsible for the physical and psychological welfare of their employees). There are instances of employers being successfully sued because they did nothing, even though they knew, about instances of bullying, harassment and/or stress (Tehrani 2001). From an organisational perspective, is working with forgiveness a worthwhile endeavour for them to even consider?

Another instance is where organisations, as such, have injured employees or customers and where there may be need for forgiveness (e.g. in Ireland, in 2001, the Christian Brothers, a teaching order of the Catholic Church, issued a public statement apologising for the hurt to many young people in their care). Organisations often fail their employees and/or their customers either directly or indirectly. Directly, there may be unjust practices around promotion and pay awards, around redundancy and redundancy packages, around reorganisational strategies; indirectly, there may be less than adequate (or no) policies in place to support or protect employees (e.g. bullying, harassment, stress, suicide, critical incident procedures). There are many 'victims of organisations' and if we include families and relationships within the ambience of organisations, then few people do not have cause for either real or imagined hurt against some institutions.

A third area where organisations wound people is teams and groups that have to face victimisation as a result of their being members of particular groups within organisations (e.g. groups who have bullied, harassed, discriminated against because of gender, race, religion, age, sexual orientation, disability). Some organisations have been designated 'institutionally racist' where racism is so built into the culture of the organisation that it imperceptibly (and often very perceptibly) imbues all aspects of work and relationships.

At work, employees are faced constantly with issues that cause them problems and give rise to such issues as forgiveness and reconciliation (e.g. bullying and harassment, poor management styles, office politics, downsizing, redundancies etc.). The hurt caused by many of these is immense. Recently, the cost of stress to industry in Britain was estimated by the Confederation of British Industry at £7 billion (*Financial Times* 1998). While this cost is astronomic, what is the cost to humans in terms of distress, illness and feelings of being uncared for, neglected and unsupported? How many people are left feeling resentful and angry at the way they have been treated by their company, firm and/or organisation? Here are some statistics that give some background to the whole area of creating potential hurt in organisations:

- More than a third of 11–16-year-old school pupils were bullied in the previous year and a quarter threatened with violence (*BBC News*, April 2000).
- Up to 5 million people in the UK feel 'very' or 'extremely' stressed by their work with half a million people believing it is making them ill (Health and Safety Executive 2002).
- UK workers work longer hours than those in any other European Union state. Some 2.7 million UK workers usually work over 48 hours per week with an average of 56 hours. This is about twice the proportion of any other European country. Recent European Union legislation has outlined the maximum number of hours that should be worked each week and a number of companies have been creative in finding ways around it.
- Forty-seven per cent of respondents to a 1999 survey had witnessed bullying at work while 10 per cent had experienced it. An estimated 18 million work days are lost each year as a result (*BBC News*, February 2000).

We have no statistics on the interpersonal conflicts at work, the stress of complaints procedures against individuals and organisations, the problems caused by poor management styles, the cost of living and working in ineffective teams, the stress and aftermath of whistle-blowing and the havoc reaped by troubled and difficult personalities within organisational contexts. Many of these result in hurt, wounded and psychologically injured individuals. What we know is that there are many, many people who are wounded as a result of their living in, working in, or being a customer of, organisations – whether these are industrial, medical, religious or educational – and that organisations themselves are poor at healing these wounds.

From the other perspective, there are organisations that have been injured through the behaviours of their personnel, employees and customers. Several Christian denominations are in deep pain because of the well-publicised instances of child abuse and paedophilia carried out by members of their ordained clergy. There are a number of government agencies suffering because of disclosures by ex-employees (e.g. MI5 and MI6) and many examples of employees stealing from their employers and selling their secrets (patents etc.) to their competitors.

Organisations, as living beings, are in need of love, care and attention and are hurt by individual, team and organisational neglect and attack. For this reason they, like individuals, need to consider forgiveness as one way of healing emotional hurts, learning and moving on, and where possible creating structures for reconciliation.

Forgiveness: individual and/or organisational

However, there are some difficulties when we begin to think of forgiveness within organisational settings. First of all, if an employee or group of employees consider themselves to be wronged (and there is need for forgiveness) by an organisation, whom do they forgive? Organisations are the people in them, and more – it is difficult to forgive an organisation as such. As Smedes (1998) points out, even if the organisation is forgiven there is usually no way it can respond, repent or be remorseful. He suggests, and there may be substance in what he writes, that 'perhaps it would be simpler if we left estrangement – between individuals and corporations – to the legal realm of contracts and compensation and limited forgiving to people *within* the corporation' (p. 347). Perhaps. On the other

hand, individuals in organisations have been known to ask forgiveness on behalf of their organisation for past deeds against individuals and groups of individuals (e.g. the Catholic Archbishop of
Paris asked forgiveness, on behalf of the Catholic Church, for the
silence of the Church during World War II on the treatment of
Jews; President Clinton has apologised for the slavery of bygone
days and to Japanese-Americans for their treatment during World
War II). Rarely do we hear organisations ask for forgiveness
from their employees, or others, for actions they have taken (e.g.
redundancy, downsizing, moving sites, cutting costs, unprofessional
practice, racism etc.). We occasionally hear individuals apologise to
organisations for letting them down or betraying their ideals (e.g.
government ministers who have resigned).

Secondly, most of the studies, research and literature on forgiveness is 'individually' based (Worthington 1998) and may not
always be applicable to organisational settings. However, what
these studies do well, and what is applicable across forgiveness
contexts, is that they isolate the meaning of forgiveness. The term
forgiveness itself is associated with other words such as hurt,
grudge, revenge, confession, reconciliation, apologies, atonement,
absolution, cancelling debts, repair and pardon. While overlapping
in meaning, it is important from the beginning that we are clear
about what forgiveness means. Enright and Coyle (1998) consider
forgiveness as an interpersonal process with three points:

1   The injured person is able to recognise an actual injustice.
2   The injured person chooses willingly and without coercion to
    respond with mercy rather than what could be justifiable
    retribution.
3   Forgiveness is decidedly moral, concerned with the good of
    human interaction.

Forgiveness is thus 'the inner surgery of the heart' (Enright and
Coyle 1998: 141), the process whereby an individual or an organisation decides to let go of an injury or a wounding for the sake of
the relationship. From the above it is clear that repentance (on the
part of the perpetrator – be they an individual or an organisation)
or reconciliation (a renewing of a past relationship) are not
prerequisites for forgiveness.

Staying with this definition proves difficult when applied to
organisations unless we restrict it to the individual who is forgiving

an organisation. It does not apply readily when organisations or communities are asked to forgive one another or when the organisation asks for forgiveness from an individual, groups or other organisations. Shriver (1995: 9) posits a description of forgiveness within political contexts, which can be used in most group or organisational environments:

> Forgiveness in a political context, then, is an act that joins moral truth, forbearance, empathy, and commitment to repair a fractured human relation. Such a combination calls for a collective turning from the past that neither ignores past evil nor excuses it, that neither overlooks justice nor reduces justice to revenge, that insists on the humanity of enemies even in their commission of dehumanising deeds, and that values the justice that restores political community above the justice that destroys it.

Such a description has value when applied to both private and public organisations and is equally as difficult to implement there as it is in the wider political field.

Factors in forgiveness within organisations

A number of factors are worth remembering when looking at organisational hurt and forgiveness. For most perpetrators of wrong, injury, hurt or indeed, evil, see themselves as not doing wrong. As Baumeister (1999: 1) points out:

> Evil usually enters the world unrecognised by the people who open the door and let it in. Evil exists primarily in the eye of the beholder, especially in the eye of the victim. If there were no victims there would be no evil . . . the question of evil is a victim's question.

This raises the question of how aware organisations are of hurting employees and customers and how easily they see 'no problem' or make it the problem of the individual. For this reason it is difficult for organisations to ask for forgiveness since they usually have lots of reasons to justify why they did what and do not see it as hurtful or injurious. The literature is replete with examples of individuals and organisations who see no harm in what is clearly very harmful to others (see Arendt 1963; Harvey 1998); Kitson and Campbell 1996). Even where there is acceptance of doing wrong, it is subject to the 'magnitude gap' where perpetrators of wrong (both individual and organisation) understate the damage they do. By and large, perpetrators of wrong, or injury, underplay either what happened to the victim, or victims, or the effects of what happened to them. A group notorious for such downplay is sex offenders who frequently deny that what they did damaged others or had any ill effects on their victims. They even make it the fault of the victim. ('She obviously meant yes when she was saying no; she wouldn't stop talking; I knew by the way she looked at me that she scorned me; I was only teaching the child how to love.')

Secondly, forgiveness entails both emotional and cognitive elements. In my mediation work in organisations I am amazed how irrelevant the 'facts' become (for further thoughts on mediation within the criminal justice system, see Chapter 6). The 'facts' get lost in the mists of time and recounting them from differing perspectives only enhances the realisation of how differently we often perceive events. By the time I deal with warring factions (individuals or teams), emotions and feelings have taken over and are driving the process. There are now two factors that require attention: the feelings of the parties and how to manage these and deal with what actually happened and how to ensure that it does not happen again. Consultants, mediators and counsellors who work in organisational settings neglect dealing with the emotional aspects of organisational life at their peril. Purely rational interventions rarely work.

Models of forgiveness in organisations

Smedes (1998) points out some of the 'quandaries' in forgiveness in organisations, one of which is that it is difficult to arrange that one group forgive another (should one take a vote?). His model of forgiveness, worked out within the individual context, has application to organisations. He suggests a four-stage model, which he envisages as four stations along the journey to hope. I will use his model as a process for forgiveness in organisations and built into it aspects from other models (Noer 1993; Enright and Coyle 1998; Worthington 1998) while adding an additional sub-stage: mediation and justice.

Stage 1: estrangement

In Stage 1, an injury is caused, or seen to be caused, which results in an estrangement between two parties (these could be individuals, or individuals and organisations, or groups within an organisation, or even communities or countries). Because of the injury or wrong done, an estrangement takes place where once there was unity, or friendship, or agreement. Clearly, estrangement is a different concept from strangeness, the latter being more connected to otherness and difference rather than an injury or wrong being done. However, being strangers can result in injuries (looking down on, prejudice towards, treating unfairly etc.). Baumeister (1999) recounts numerous ways in which evil enters the world through a 'them . . . us' mentality. Once we envisage them as 'them, and not us', then we are in a strong position to injure them, especially if we can depict them as the enemy. It is easy to see how estrangement as a result of injury or wrong can take place in organisations for many of the reasons mentioned above (unfair appraisal systems, discrimination, harassment, downsizing etc.) and especially in regard to the 'psychological contract' outlined above. A number of factors enter at this stage of development that either polarise the people involved or move them on to a further stage. Polarisation takes place when:

- The victim is blamed for the injury (it's your own fault, you brought it on yourself, somebody needed to tell you the truth).
- Communication breaks down or becomes overly rational. The parties give up talking to each other or communication becomes written, impersonal and not emotional. Noer (1993) posits communication as the first stage in 'healing wounds'.
- Emotions are not dealt with but are forced underground. There is no recognition of the feelings of the victim (whether that victim is individual or an organisation), sometimes by the victim themselves, but most often by the perpetrators or others. (Why are you getting so upset? Is it really us you are angry with? We will get nowhere if we continue to be emotional.) Not dealing effectively with emotions (grow up, don't be childish, pull yourself together) only exacerbates the divide.
- There is no attempt at recalling and reviewing the situation. A refusal to talk about it (we've tried and got nowhere) and/or refusal to recall (it's all in the past and why rake it up, it

happened three years ago, we have moved on since then) leaves the victim responsible for holding the grudge, irrationally!

Consultants, counsellors and mediators can help move the episode on to the next phase by facilitating:

- A recognition that someone or an organisation is hurt and a willingness to give time and energy to talking about it with the relevant people.
- Dealing with the emotional side of the injury and allowing expression of feelings (whether these are feelings of hurt, shame, anger, betrayal etc.). These emotional expressions can be articulated by the organisation where it is hurt (e.g. a group of priests expressing their anger with colleagues who have betrayed them through sexual abuse).
- Articulation of what happened and how it is perceived from many sides.
- A willingness to build in repair of the injury and in organisations, in particular, a willingness to look at policies and strategies that might mean such events do not occur in the future (e.g. bullying policy, suicide policy).

In Stage 1 (Station 1), it is vital to acknowledge what has happened, how people and groups and organisations feel about what has happened (what actually happened or perceptions of what happened) and begin to allow expression and articulation of this as well as building a base of willingness to do something about it. Working with individuals and teams is particularly effective at this stage especially in facilitating expression of feelings. Consultants, mediators and/or counsellors usually come in at this stage – when there is recognition that estrangement had taken place and something needs to be done about it. Without that awareness, there is little that can be done and those who intervene have to go back and create an insight into the need for intervention.

Stage 1a: mediation and justice

This is a sub-station (or sub-stage) not mentioned by Smedes. Here, I believe, is the opportunity to look at justice and mediation that come before forgiveness. Moving from Station 1 (it is possible to get stuck there forever, of course) means reviewing what happened from a perspective of justice and fairness. Can we set up an independent body (e.g. truth and reconciliation committee, an independent mediator) to help ascertain what happened and in so far as is possible, repair and make good the damage which has been caused?

Here, there will be understanding of where the injury comes from (from within the individual, from relationships, from the organisation itself). A good assessment enables the helper to ensure that they are not asking too much from the individual or making too many psychological assumptions. A client who is being sexually harassed or discriminated against regarding promotion needs to be helped to see that these issues are external and need to be tackled as external problems and not simply as internal ones.

Reviewing interventions to help the person deal with their own contribution to the injuries in their lives (if this is appropriate and apt) is also appropriate here. Understanding oneself may indeed be a first step in all forgiveness, and organisational self-understanding is crucial in seeing how problems may be created. I need to forgive myself for being narcissistic and asking everyone to look to my needs, for being selfish and inconsiderate at times, for not working hard enough to deserve promotion or a pay rise and then reacting negatively when I do not get one. Organisations can do the same and review how they sometimes are the cause of the problems they create (e.g. poor management training and styles, lack of suitable procedures and policies, not tackling institutional norms). What is, or is not, my (our) contribution to what happens is a fair question (realising that I may not have contributed to what happened, e.g. a sexual attack).

Where there are instances of conflict or disagreement, the 'facts' very easily get lost in the emotions that overwhelm. Helping people deal with the emotions of what happened is as important, and in many instances more important, than dealing with the facts of what took place.

The hope is that this station may emerge with some independent (objective!) factors that may move the situation towards some conclusion acceptable to both sides. Noer (1993) sees dealing with emotions as the second stage in his model of helping survivors of downsizing. It is important that emotions are not privatised (Whitehead and Whitehead 1994) but socialised – i.e. relocated where they belong. All people involved are allowed to express feelings and Noer suggests groups as one of the best ways to help facilitate emotional release. Group facilitators can be of great benefit here.

In this stage of mediation and justice strategies and interventions can include:

- articulating and dealing with actual events and setting up mediation facilities;
- apologies, when appropriate;
- counselling to help victims find a voice for themselves;
- coaching/mentoring programmes for perpetrators to help with insights into why they victimise and how they can learn to behave differently;
- compensation, when appropriate;
- strategies for changing organisational culture (racist, sexist, macho, etc.);
- team development events;
- training in giving and receiving feedback;
- training for managers in recognising signs of stress.

Stage 1a concentrates on articulating what happens and seeing if ways through can be found (mediation and justice). It also looks to longer-term strategies as ways of ensuring similar events do not reoccur.

Stage 2: forgiveness

Smedes (1998) presents Stage 2 as forgiveness and sees three elements within it: (a) discovering the humanity of the offender; (b) surrendering the right to get even; and (c) changing one's feelings towards the offender. Discovering the humanity of the offender means separating *what* they did from *who* they are ('What the offender *did* becomes what the offender *is*', Smedes 1998: 344). With respect to organisations, the victim begins to see that the organisation is not all evil or bad but made up of individuals, like himself or herself, who are weak and fallible. The victim realises that people in organisational settings often regress to producing infantile behaviour.

Giving up the right for justice or revenge, or getting even, is quite a difficult stance to take in organisations, especially where there have been injustices, broken promises, unfairness etc.

In the final element, the victim changes his or her feelings towards the perpetrator and moves towards a more kindly attitude. Here Smedes points out some of the limitations of forgiveness: it is individual (not social), it takes only one person (not two or more), it is unconditional and it can happen without reconciliation. However, these may not necessarily be drawbacks and organisations can begin to think communally.

To begin the process of forgiveness one first has to empathise. Lack of empathy is one of the main reasons why individuals perpetrate such cruelty on others (Baumeister 1999). Empathy is not just a valuable asset from the victim's perspective but also from the point of view of the perpetrator. It is of immense help to victims for others (perpetrator included) to show that they now understand what it means from the victim's viewpoint. Employee assistance programmes (EAPs) can offer help here, as can internal counselling services.

There also needs to be realisation that forgiveness is a gift given by the victim rather than a right of the perpetrator. Even when justice has been done (e.g. a victim of sexual abuse sees the perpetrator jailed, a victim of unfair dismissal is returned to the job) individuals are left with the events that happened and still have to come to terms with them. Forgiveness enters the frame when other strategies to let go (even after justice has been seen to be done) still no longer work. In a paradoxical way, forgiveness is what works when nothing else works – it is the final mode of emotional healing if all else fails. It does not have to reach such a final stage and can enter the process earlier (even being a beginning response) but for many it is the intervention used when others have failed.

Finally it must be understood that forgiveness is a process and that, usually, the commitment to forgive is the beginning of that process, not the end: it takes time for forgiveness to work and permeate the system. Forgiveness needs to be held onto over time and remade again and again.

At Stage 2, victims begin the process of forgiving and those victims can be individuals or organisations. This process can take place with or without the cooperation of the perpetrator.

Stage 3: reconciliation

Forgiveness and reconciliation are not the same but the hope is that one will lead to the other. However, forgiveness has value even when the end result is not reconciliation. And there are different levels of reconciliation: reunion, cool coexistence, tolerance etc. But reconciliation, unlike forgiveness, is conditional and one of these conditions is remorse on the part of the perpetrator. Mediation and conflict resolution within organisations can be a valuable tool towards reconciliation and can help all parties begin to think of how they work and live together personally and professionally. Isaacs' work on dialogue can be of help here (1999). He suggests that we learn best (and this seems to apply to reconciliation) when we give up 'certainty' and move into questioning the assumptions we bring to what we are certain about. In suspending our own certainty we are able to hear what others have to say. And we move towards respect for others and their truth. Respecting them does not mean agreeing with them but allowing them to speak *their* truth. We give 'voices' to what needs to be said. Honesty, transparency and congruence allow us to move forward as we search for ways of talking and 'thinking together'.

The result is a movement from monologue through skilful conversation (debate, argument) to dialogue (beginning to reflect together). Noer (1993) calls this the stage of 'breaking co-dependency' where relationships are renegotiated so that one person (victim or perpetrator, in this case) does not establish a relationship with the other, be that other an organisation or not, that keeps that person dependent on the other. Noer points out that many organisations pull their employees into a 'co-dependent' relationship with them that allows for hurt and injury to take place. Where one person annexes their happiness to another or to an organisation then, according to Noer, co-dependency exists. Here again, counsellors who work in organisations, either in-house or as EAP associates, can help by inviting clients to look at their relationship with the organisation. They can also help organisations look at how their policies, procedures and overall culture pull employees into certain kinds of relationships with them, some of which are not healthy for either party.

Stage 4: hope

While forgiveness begins the process of reconciliation, hope creates the moral energy to pursue it (Smedes 1998: 353). In dialogue, new possibilities emerge but this means that both parties suspend certainty and begin a new journey without the certainties or the memories of the past. Isaacs (1999) illustrates how 'memory' captures us in the past in ways that imprison us. He equates memory with 'thoughts' rather than with 'thinking', the latter freeing us from what memory has stabilised and frozen. Hope sees the person anew, leaves aside the old memories (without forgetting them) and turns to begin anew with a 'stranger' look (he suggests that we make the familiar other into a stranger-other as a way of learning from them anew). The victim and the perpetrator both give each other 'second looks' – the 'first look' has been that established in memory, the second look takes a different and less familiar stance and so is the look of hope. In organisations it is possible to see how this might be as we turn from our certainties, our assumptions, our expectations, our projections and our beliefs to meet the firm, the hospital, the school, the workplace again and give it the second look of hope. We can then begin a new dialogue.

At Stage 4, hope is generated through a number of strategies used by consultants, mediators and counsellors:

- We learn from what has happened. All parties, individuals and organisations ask: what have we learned from this experience? Not opening what has happened to learning may result in repetition of events. (Those who do not learn from history are condemned to repeating it.)
- Policies are formulated to enshrine our commitment to changing what has happened so that it may not happen again.
- Strategies are put in place to ensure no repetitions. These strategies will take place at both individual and organisational level (e.g. training some employees in how to deal with bullying episodes and having a policy on harassment in place).
- The kinds of relationships within the organisation as a whole are reviewed and movement towards a new system of relating (not co-dependent) is implemented. Part of this review will be a realisation, in more detail, of the 'shadow side' of organisations and how this side can impact behaviour within the organisation (Egan 1994). Noer (1993) calls this the 'systemic' side of the renewal process where new relationships between all parties are renegotiated.

A further element of hope is that it actually finds meaning in what has happened. Many people make sense of what has happened in their lives, albeit that what has happened has been negative, by reframing it to help others. So victims of bullying in one organisation set up a confidential helpline, with the support of the organisation, to help those who need someone to talk to about being bullied at work. We see further organisational examples of this in the Suzy Lamplugh Trust and Alcoholics Anonymous (AA) where individuals who have suffered move on to create organisations to help those who have suffered similar experiences.

Conclusion

Can we ask, and should we ask, organisations to forgive and ask for forgiveness? Should we help and facilitate individuals to forgive organisations that have injured them or disappointed them? Psychologically, it makes sense. Not just for individuals, so that they can let go and get on with their lives, not just for organisations, so that they can learn how to deal more sensibly with the humans that make up their workforce, but because forgiveness itself, no matter where it takes place, heals hearts and remakes relationships. With forgiveness, new dimensions of human endeavour enter the workplace, courage and heroism are displayed and generosity beyond what is normally possible takes place. Forgiveness pulls us, and our organisations, beyond . . .

References

Arendt, H. (1963) *Eichmann in Jerusalem: A Report on the Banality of Evil.* Harmondsworth: Penguin.

Baumeister, R.F. (1999) *Evil: Inside Human Violence and Cruelty.* New York: W.H. Freeman.

De Geus, A. (1997) *The Living Company: Growth, Learning and Longevity in Business.* London: Nicholas Brealey.

Egan, G. (1994) *Working the Shadow Side: A Guide to Positive Behind the Scenes Management.* San Francisco: Jossey-Bass.

Enright, R.D. and Coyle, C.T. (1998) Researching the process model of forgiveness within psychological interventions, in E.L. Worthington (ed.) *Dimensions of Forgiveness.* Radnor, PA: Templeton Foundation Press.

Harvey, J. (1988) *The Abilene Paradox and Other Meditations on Management.* San Francisco: Jossey-Bass.

Hinshelwood, R.D. (2001) *Thinking about Institutions.* London: Jessica Kingsley.

Isaacs, W. (1999) *Dialogue and the Art of Thinking Together: A Pioneering*

Approach to Communication in Business and in Life. San Francisco: Jossey-Bass.

Kitson, A. and Campbell, R. (1996) *The Ethical Organisation: Ethical Theory and Corporate Behaviour.* London: Macmillan.

Makin, P., Cooper, C. and Cox, C. (1996) *Organisations and the Psychological Contract.* Leicester: British Psychological Society.

Noer, D. (1993) *Healing the Wounds: How to Revitalise Downsized Organisations.* San Francisco: Jossey-Bass.

Shriver, D.W. (1995) *An Ethic for Enemies: Forgiveness in Politics.* New York: Oxford University Press.

Smedes, L.B. (1998) Stations on the journey from forgiveness to hope, in E.L. Worthington (ed.) *Dimensions of Forgiveness.* Radnor, PA: Templeton Foundation Press.

Smith, B. and Yanowitz, J. (1999) Sustainable innovation, in P. Senge, A. Kleiner, C. Roberts, R. Ross, G. Roth and B. Smith (eds) *The Dance of Change.* London: Nicholas Brealey.

Tehrani, N. (2001) *Building a Culture of Respect: Managing Bullying at Work.* London: Taylor & Francis.

Whitehead, J.D. and Whitehead, E. (1994) *Shadows of the Heart: A Spirituality of Negative Emotions.* New York: Crossroad.

Worthington, E.L. (ed.) (1998) *Dimensions of Forgiveness.* Radnor, PA: Templeton Foundation Press.

Chapter 6

Transformation, healing or forgiveness? Assisting victims of crime through restorative practice

Guy Masters

Introduction

In this chapter I will describe, briefly, the emergence of an international movement within the criminal justice field commonly referred to as 'restorative justice'. I will cover the reasons why this movement has emerged, how it operates in practice, describe some of the underlying academic theories that have become associated with restorative justice, and the links that are beginning to be made with the emerging field of forgiveness therapy. I have personally been involved in the restorative justice field since 1993, when introduced to it by David Smith, who was my PhD supervisor at Lancaster University. At that time, as a criminology student, I was strongly drawn to restorative justice as it represented the only positive activity within the very bleak landscape of criminology and criminal justice policy. Of particular fascination to me was that restorative justice seemed to show that people, who had either committed sometimes quite terrible crimes or suffered them, were capable of meeting with one another to resolve what had happened. I was also drawn to the significant benefits that restorative practices appeared to have for crime victims.

This chapter is predominantly academic and descriptive; however, it also includes a small number of accounts from my own experience as a restorative justice practitioner. As will become clear, while forgiveness can be of significance to crime victims, I personally do not believe that it should be a central aim for restorative practice. However, I will consider the arguments, from within the forgiveness therapy field, that forgiveness is something that crime victims explicitly seek to achieve.

The development of restorative practice

Since the 1970s the criminal justice systems of many countries have been increasingly criticised for the way in which they treat victims of crime (Mawby and Walklate 1994). Victims commonly complain that they are treated with little compassion, kept poorly informed, and often feel that they are regarded principally as pieces of evidence (see Giuliano 1998) for many vivid descriptions by victims of their experience of the criminal justice process). Many people feel that they are victimised further by the criminal justice system that is supposed to deliver them justice. Critics argue that the principal reason for this occurring is that most criminal justice systems are primarily orientated toward the prosecution of offenders, who may then be punished and/or assisted (Zehr 1990). Offences are primarily seen as a violation of the laws of the state, and the state then represents the actual victim, often effectively alienating them through this process. Once the state has passed sentence, the case is considered closed, leaving many victims feeling angry, bitter, and with no sense of closure. Indeed, many victims never even know that the case actually went to court.

It never ceases to amaze or disappoint me how, even today, very few victims actually receive any information at all about what has happened. For example, I have recently been working with a young female victim of assault, whose school uniform was taken by the police as it could provide vital forensic evidence if any of the offenders (three in this case) pleaded not guilty. During the assault, the girl had been spat on and forensic tests could be used to prove the case. The girl and her mother were very concerned that there might be a trial requiring the young victim to give evidence. They both feared it would be a further traumatic experience. In reality, all three offenders pleaded guilty and no trial was necessary. However, when I contacted the victim's mother some six weeks after the offenders had been sentenced, they had still not been told that all three had been to court, pleaded guilty and hence there would not be a trial. Furthermore, they had no idea how to go about recovering the uniform from the police (which we did for them).

Since the late 1970s one (of several) movements that has grown considerably and sought to deliver a greater sense of justice for victims is now commonly referred to as 'restorative justice'. Within restorative justice a crime is no longer seen as primarily an offence committed against the state, but is considered to be a violation of people and relationships, causing varying levels of harm to different people. Restorative responses seek to identify the full extent and nature of this harm, and look to repair this as much as possible. Within restorative justice, rehabilitative assistance would still be given to offenders considered in need (this can be interpreted as an attempt to restore the offenders) and those offenders considered to be a significant menace would still be incarcerated to protect society. However, probably the most significant difference within restorative justice is the way in which victims are treated. Victims should be dealt with sympathetically, and their needs should be assessed and met as far as possible.

Restorative justice has become an international and diverse social movement, based around some identifiable fundamental values (see Bazemore and Walgrave 2000). However, full exploration of the philosophical and theoretical beliefs within restorative justice is beyond the scope of this chapter. The primary focus for the remainder of this chapter is twofold. First, I will chart the significant developments to have occurred within restorative practice and note the impact that this practice appears to have upon victims of crime. Second, these findings will be discussed in relation to some established models of assisting people suffering from post-traumatic stress disorder (Bard and Sangrey 1986; Herman 1992), and emerging models of forgiveness therapy (Enright and Fitzgibbons 2000).

Early developments in restorative practice: victim-offender reconciliation

The first orchestrated attempt to deliver what is now described as restorative justice was in Ontario, Canada. This was brought about by a Mennonite group who had been discussing how to increase the practice of Christian values within the criminal justice system and the use of community volunteers. A probation officer, who was part of the Mennonite group, proposed to the judge in a vandalism case that the two young adult offenders responsible for the offences meet with the 22 victims to work out how to repay them. The judge supported this approach and, as part of a probation order, the two offenders met with the majority of the victims and agreed how to repay their losses. Further early successes led to the formation of a

'Victim-Offender Reconciliation Project' (VORP), in Kitchener, Ontario, in 1975, to carry out such practice on a systematic basis, primarily with property offences (Peachey 1989).

Within VORP, the main vehicle for attempting reconciliation was to offer victims and offenders the opportunity to meet with each other through mediation. The actual practice of mediation has developed with experience and now usually progresses in the following way. Both offender and victim are offered the opportunity to meet voluntarily with each other in the presence of a mediator. If they agree, meetings usually take place following some preparation work, when the mediators judge the parties to be ready. The purpose of the meeting is usually twofold. First, it is an opportunity for the victim and the offender to discuss the offence. Victims can explain how the offence affected them and see the offender's reactions to this. They may be able to learn more about why the offence occurred and about the offender as a person. They get the opportunity to ask specific questions about the offence, which the offender may be able to answer. Second, the two can consider if, and how, the offender can make up for the harm done – for example, through compensating the victim for any losses. This 'restitution' or 'reparation' may be financial, or may be through offenders undertaking work directly for the victim, though it is more usual for them to do work for a third party, commonly a charity. Sometimes, victims only ask the offender not to commit any more offences, or to seek to improve their lives (Wright 1996).

The experience in Ontario demonstrated that many victims and offenders, given the opportunity, would meet with one other, and could successfully arrange reparation. While this project was never subjected to any formal evaluation, its publicised experience, and that of other projects that sought to mediate in civil cases, encouraged the establishment of similar projects, particularly in the USA. Some of these later projects did not limit themselves to non-violent property offences and demonstrated that mediation could take place even when the offence was of a serious violent nature, though such cases often require greater preparation work by the mediator (Umbreit 1989). In the 1980s a number of European countries also established similar projects, working with both property and violent offences. Evaluations of these projects demonstrated mixed, but generally favourable, results (Marshall and Merry 1990; Davis 1992). Many victims were shown to have benefited from their involvement, some quite dramatically. Victims who participated were found to be more satisfied with the criminal justice system, have a greater sense that justice had been done, and had reduced fears of re-victimisation (Umbriet and Roberts 1996). Though it has yet to be formally quantified, there are a significant number of examples which illustrate that some victims can gain a great deal through mediation, as demonstrated by the following case study (Mediation UK 1994: 13).

Burglary

A victim support service requested that a burglary victim meet a burglar. The victim was having difficulty sleeping and suspected all strangers, including people at the bus stop outside her house. She had received considerable support from victim support, but still had many questions as to why her house had been chosen. A meeting was arranged between her, her husband and the burglar who had wanted to apologise to his victims, but had been unable to do so.

The meeting took place in the prison where the burglar was serving a three and a half year sentence for two burglaries. The victim was able to ask all her questions and felt reassured by the offender's answers because he responded honestly, and also seemed genuinely concerned about what had happened to her. After the meeting, she was able to sleep well again and go back to her normal activities and way of life. She only wished that the meeting could have taken place a lot earlier, to set her mind at rest.

My own experiences verify this. Though I am also aware that – as well as the process of meeting the offender and having the chance to ask critical questions – simply hearing from an official within the criminal justice system that what happened is being taken seriously and what this means in practice in relation to the offender, can be hugely reassuring for victims. A male victim of a vicious assault, with whom I worked, seemed far more impressed with the fact that, within two days of being sentenced at court, the young offender had been assessed by a clinical psychologist and begun a mandatory anger management course, than with any answers the offender could give about the offence. The victim had assumed that, as the offender was not yet considered to be an adult, 'nothing would happen'.

Developments in restorative practice: from reconciliation to communication

I have already stated that the first VORP was guided by religious beliefs that part of the response to a criminal offence should be to attempt reconciliation between the parties: the mending of ruptured relationships. While I have noted that it is difficult to evaluate the extent to which reconciliation has occurred between victims and offenders (Peachey 1989), much research has examined the reasons why victims and offenders participate, and what benefits and drawbacks are identified by them. One of the first empirical evaluations of the VORP model (Coates and Gehm 1989) found the main reasons why victims took part were:

- to recover their losses
- to help offenders stay out of further trouble and
- to participate meaningfully in the process.

The reasons offenders gave were to avoid harsher punishment, to get the experience behind them and to make amends to their victims. Victims reported being satisfied by four things:

- the opportunity to meet the offender and gain a better understanding of the offence and the offender
- the opportunity to receive restitution
- the expression of some remorse from the offender and finally
- the care and attention that they received from the mediator.

Interestingly, this evaluation found that reconciliation between victims and the offenders appeared to occur in approximately a third of mediated cases, though it should be noted that the definition of reconciliation used by these researchers was whether the people involved came to see each other as people and not merely as objects or stereotypes (Coates and Gehm 1989: 255) – i.e. that some *connection* occurred between the parties as people. Obviously, as many offenders and victims are strangers, it is not the same, as in much of the forgiveness field, where reconciliation is about *reconnection*. Indeed, for many people in my experience it is enough to hear that the offender has expressed remorse for their actions, illustrating that they have the ability to recognise their actions as unacceptable. Thus, while the desire for a process which could achieve reconciliation between victims and offenders was a driving goal for many initial project developers, evaluation quickly established that this was of lesser importance to many victims who took part, only occurring in a minority of cases.

This finding has been verified by further research (e.g. Marshall and Merry 1990; Umbreit 1994), which has identified that the foremost benefit for victims is the sense of empowerment provided by restorative justice processes, with many victims appreciating the opportunity to be meaningfully involved in the criminal justice process, and to be able to express their opinions and emotions about the offence. Umbreit (1994: 95) found that, for a quarter of victims, empowerment led to some sense of healing, resolving some feelings of grief and distress caused by the crime. While it may not be too surprising that reconciliation is not a common aim for people who had no prior relationship with each other, there are examples of instances where relationships are forged between victims and offenders. For example, Braithwaite and Mugford (1994: 149) state that:

> Some reconciliations are quite remarkable. The most extra-ordinary case we know of involved a young man guilty of aggravated assault with a firearm on a woman who ran a lotto shop. The offender locked the woman at gunpoint in the back of her shop while he robbed her of over $1000. When the time for the conference came, she was mad, after blood. Yet after considerable discussion, part of the plan of action, fully agreed to by the victim, involved the victim housing the offender while he did some community work for her family!

However, as experience illustrated that reconciliation was neither the main aim, nor benefit, for the majority of people who participated, practitioners began to use the terms 'mediation' or 'dialogue' in place of 'reconciliation'. This represents a significant shift for practitioners. The aim of achieving reconciliation was replaced by providing opportunities for involvement and communication in the criminal justice system. Other restorative justice models have now also been developed which seek to involve wider groups of individuals who have been affected by an offence. For example, 'family group conferencing' and 'restorative conferencing' models seek to involve the families and friends of both victims and offenders in meetings (see Mediation UK 2001 for a comprehensive review of different restorative justice models), though mediation remains the most widely used model.

Links between restorative justice and criminological theory

It is worth noting that the development of the restorative conferencing model was strongly informed by John Braithwaite's criminological theory of 'reintegrative shaming'. Braithwaite's (1989) theory argues that in order to prevent reoffending the offender should be made to feel shame for what they have done, but not be stigmatised by this process. Shaming is necessary to indicate that the behaviour is unacceptable, but orchestrated in such a manner that the offender is aware that they are not considered a bad person and are able to remain/regain being a full member of the law abiding community. Consequently, conferences, with offenders attending accompanied by family and friends, have been labelled as 'ceremonies' of shaming and reintegration (Braithwaite and Mugford 1994) – though the less structured VORP model can also achieve this, it was not an explicit aim. Many facilitators of this model follow a standard script which sets out the questions to be asked of participants, *and their order*. This script is designed to bring about a discussion of the material and emotional impact of the offending for the victims, the offenders and those close to both. I have found this script particularly useful with younger offenders who are very nervous and also when victims have expressed a desire to meet the offender(s) but are unsure what they particularly wish to know.

At the beginning of a conference the offender is asked to describe in some detail what happened, their thoughts and feelings at the time of the offence, and since. Victims, their supporters, and those present in support of the offender are also asked to describe the offence and its impact from their perspective, again focusing on their feelings at the time of the offence and subsequently. This is intended to reveal to the offender the full harm they have caused. Offenders are given the opportunity to respond to what has been said, commonly by acknowledging the harm they have caused, and expressing remorse and regret for that. The supporters of the offender are then asked to comment on whether this sort of behaviour is common or not, and whether they are usually a good person etc. The conference will also consider whether any action needs to be taken by the offender to make up for the harm that has been caused. This conferencing model has been the subject of considerable further theorising about what emotional process is necessary to 'restore' or 'transform' all who are present. This will be considered in detail later in this chapter, as it has become evident that 'dealing with shame' may well be as relevant to victims as it is to offenders.

The role of forgiveness within restorative justice: theory and reality

I personally find it very difficult to discuss the topic of forgiveness in relation to restorative justice. Some advocates argue that for-giveness does have a clear role, but I am unsure. For example, Dickey (1998: 107) contends that 'apology, forgiveness, and restitution are important components of any restoration or healing that occurs'. Howard Zehr (1990: 45), one of the most influential writers on restorative justice, makes a similar point: 'for genuine healing to take place, at least two preconditions need to be met: repentance and forgiveness. If healing is to occur, it is helpful for victims to be able to forgive'. Zehr acknowledges that, from a theological perspective, this is theoretically straightforward as God requires that we forgive our enemies and those that hurt us. However, from a practical perspective, forgiveness, particularly in cases of serious offences, is no straightforward issue. Zehr and Dickey are both clear that to suggest that victims of crime might forgive those who have harmed them is not to suggest that victims simply forget about or condone what happened. Zehr (1990: 47) states that:

> Forgiveness is letting go of the power the offense and the offender have over a person. It means no longer letting that offense and offender dominate. Without this experience of forgiveness, without this closure, the wound festers, the viola-tion takes over our consciousness, our lives. It, and the offender, are in control. Real forgiveness, then, is an act of empowerment and healing. It allows one to move from victim to survivor.

It is apparent then that forgiveness is an end-point, demarcating the 'closure' of the incident for the victim, perhaps best understood as the significant diminishment of negative feelings. I have already noted that there are examples of 'transformational' stories of healing within the literature on restorative justice. However I think it is necessary to question how representative these are of what commonly occurs through restorative practice. Kathy Daly (2000) is perhaps the most critical commentator in regard to this, arguing that many commentators on restorative justice (admittedly myself included) have presented 'nirvana' stories of ideals, but not the reality. Daly's research on family group conferencing in South Australia estimated that 'nirvana like' transformational meetings occur in perhaps 10 per cent of cases, with a further 40 per cent of conferences ending on a good note. In a comprehensive review of the known research evidence for victims of crime (Masters 2001), I identified a common pattern among restorative justice pro- grammes. A majority of victims (60–70 per cent) do appear to benefit from participation, having reduced levels of anger, anxiety and fear of further victimisation. However, participation often did not relieve all of the concerns of victims, and for a minority of victims appears to make these worse. Consequently, I agree with Daly (2000) that caution must be taken when advocating restora- tive approaches. They do not hold all of the answers, and oppor- tunities for dialogue with offenders should be seen as just one possible way of assisting victims.

The impact of crime for victims

The impact that crimes have upon victims varies considerably so it is difficult to make generalisations about how victims are affected. While it can be said that more serious offences are likely to have a more profound and longer lasting impact on victims, it is also dangerous to assume that seemingly minor offences will have little impact. Maguire and Corbett (1987), in their landmark study on the effects of crime, found that a substantial proportion of victims of offences often regarded as 'minor', notably threats and criminal damage offences, are significantly affected. Victims are most affected in the hours and days following the offence. However, the majority of victims recover quite quickly and few report still being affected several weeks after the offence.

For example, 78 per cent of victims of burglary, robbery, assault and theft, who received no support, other than from friends and family, reported that they were affected either very much or quite a lot in the first few hours following the offence. This had fallen to 37 per cent three to six weeks later. Those victims reporting that they were 'not at all' affected had increased from 0 to 20 per cent. The most common reactions that are reported by victims are feeling angry (55 per cent), feeling unsettled or uneasy (37 per cent), feeling frightened (36 per cent), having difficulty sleeping (36 per cent), feeling dazed, confused or unreal (35 per cent). Twenty-five per cent report being unable to do ordinary tasks, losing interest in their work or hobbies and being depressed. Twenty-four per cent lose their appetite, 23 per cent are afraid to go out and 16 per cent report feeling or being sick, and not wanting to be alone.

A year after the offence, around 8 per cent of victims report still being significantly affected by the offence. This masks some considerable variations, with 15 per cent of burglary victims and 25 per cent of victims of woundings, robbery or snatch thefts reporting that they are still significantly affected. The most prevalent continuing psychological effects reported by victims of robbery, assault and snatch thefts are persistent thoughts about the crime, anger and fear of going out.

These victims also report feeling less cheerful, 'less warm to other people' and having 'less energy'. Forty per cent reported that they now went out less, and avoided certain places. Over a quarter reported that they had not got any better in the previous three months and 7 per cent reported that they were getting worse. Over 20 per cent of victims reported that they thought the offence would have a very strong effect on their life in the future (Maguire and Corbett 1987).

The effects of the most serious assault offences, and rape, profoundly affect significant numbers of victims, and these effects are often long lasting, with many victims retaining serious symptoms for many years (Maguire and Corbett 1987). Shapland et al.s (1985) longitudinal study of 276 victims of serious offences found that the majority of them suffered from some kind of emotional effect, which often led to changes in their behaviour and lives. These were long lasting, some for years, and took the form of nervousness, anxiety and worry. Sexual assault victims were the most likely to suffer from multiple and persistent effects, with the added stress of also having to deal with the effects of the offence upon males close to them, who often treat them differently, sometimes encouraging feelings of guilt. Shapland et al. found that two and a half years after the offence some 40 per cent of victims were still suffering from a psychological or social effect because of the offence.

Trauma and victims of crime

For most people then, being a victim of crime does not lead to any prolonged psychological harm; it is an inconvenience, rather than a trauma. There is broad agreement among experts that victims recover in stages (usually three or four) from the effects of a crime, though these stages are not clearly demarcated.

Bard and Sangrey (1986) describe a three-stage process through which crime victims fluctuate. The first 'impact phase' of the crisis reaction is characterised by victims feeling disorganised, vulnerable, helpless and shocked. This phase can last as little as a few hours or much longer. Victims can be greatly assisted, at this point, by the provision of non-judgemental support enabling them to talk about how they are feeling, being reassured that their reactions are normal and by the provision of help to enable them to feel safe. In the second 'recoil phase', victims struggle to integrate their experience into their lives. Some will be greatly affected by the offence, having their entire sense of self shattered by the event. At this stage victims will commonly feel fear, anger, sadness, self-pity and guilt. They may also try to detach themselves to avoid being overwhelmed by the intense level of their feelings. Victims may suffer phobic reactions due to certain specifics of the offence, linked to specific places or times of day.

In order to progress through this stage victims must face their feelings about the incident, reliving the crime, perhaps many times. Victims may 'replay' the incident in their mind, and/or may need to talk about it a great deal. They may also fantasise and talk about a desire for revenge. However, intense feelings will eventually dissipate. A further key element of this stage which is experienced by almost all victims is to try to construct a reason why they became a victim. This draws on what is commonly described as the 'just world hypothesis'. Generally, most people have a belief that the world is somehow a just place, good and bad things only happen to those who deserve them. Being the innocent victim of a criminal offence shatters this belief. Herman (1992: 51) summarises this reaction as follows:

Traumatic events call into question basic human relationships. They breach the attachments of family, friendship, love and community. They shatter the construction of the self that is formed and sustained in relation to others. They undermine the belief systems that give meaning to human experience. They violate the victim's faith in a natural or divine order and cast the victim into a state of existential crisis.

Some victims become obsessed with the questions 'Why me? What did I do to deserve this? Could I have prevented this?' Consequently, the final stage of the crisis reaction involves victims rebuilding their sense of self. They come to accept what happened to them, their feelings diminish (but do not necessarily disappear entirely) and they become able to focus their energies on other things. This final stage can be very difficult for victims, sometimes bringing about intense feelings of guilt and shame, as one answer to the question of 'Why me?' is to erroneously blame themselves, believing they deserved to become a victim for some reason. Unfortunately the reactions of those close to the victim often exacerbate self-blame, as family and friends ask why the victim left a window open, were carrying so much money or did not cry for help etc.

Many readers will recognise this cycle as that experienced by people suffering from post-traumatic stress disorder (PTSD) with which counselling can offer effective help. In her work on PTSD, Herman (1992: 181) considers how 'integration not exorcism' is essential for individuals to recover. Following Mollica (1988: 312), the 'trauma story' needs to be transformed into a new story, 'no longer about shame and humiliation' but 'about dignity and virtue'. Consequently, telling the 'trauma story' leads to a change in how victims process the memory, and 'with this transformation of memory comes relief of many of the major symptoms of post-traumatic stress disorder' (Herman 1992: 183). This process has evocatively been described by Howard Zehr (2000) as a 'journey to belonging'.

The trauma story and restorative justice

Storytelling is an integral part of all of the restorative processes described earlier. In mediation, both victims and offenders are often given 'uninterrupted time' at the beginning of the mediation to 'tell their story' (Umbreit 1998). They will also have been asked to do this with the mediator during the preparation phase for the mediation. In the restorative/scripted conferencing model, the victims are explicitly asked to describe what happened to them, and their thoughts and feelings at the time of the offence, and since then. Given this, one difficult issue for practitioners is that many victims will decline the offer of mediation etc., precisely because they wish to avoid reliving these emotions (Marshall and Merry 1990), even though it may be their best route to relieving them.

There is evidence that such (traumatic) storytelling by victims within restorative processes does lead to the transformation described by Herman (1992). Maxwell and Morris (1993: 118), in their evaluation of Family Group Conferencing (FGC) in New Zealand, report that for some victims 'meeting with the offender was seen as a cathartic experience; negative feelings about the offence could be released'. They quote short comments from three victims: 'I got the ill feelings out of my system', 'It was very good to be able to air my feelings', 'It made me feel better; that I got my message across'. Strang and Sherman (1997: 3) provide the following account from a victim who took part in a restorative conference:

> I had this enormous amount of anger that I wanted to shout out, but I felt very defensive. I was so angry that I was sitting there literally shaking. I was able to say all the things I'd been thinking about for all those weeks and explain how angry I was . . . to put him in the picture of how it affected us made me feel so much better . . . I felt a great sense of relief of getting it off my chest.

Daly (2002) concludes from her research on conferences in serious offences that meeting offenders in conferences can have positive benefits, notably in reducing victims' anger and fear. This is also a common finding with mediation (Umbreit 1994; Umbreit and Roberts 1996). However, it should also be noted that participation in a conference or mediation does not lead to *full* recovery for many victims, but that negative emotions can be greatly reduced. Daly (2002) who has conducted the only research to date exploring this issue, found that the passing of time, the support of friends and families, and the personal resources of the victim were of equal importance in recovery. It would be highly surprising if participation in a restorative process was all that was needed to relieve traumatisation. It is indisputable, however, that the majority of victims do benefit in some way, and that these processes are far more beneficial to victims than those whose offenders are prosecuted in court (Strang 2000).

The role of shame

I have already stated that victimisation often leads to intense feelings of humiliation, shame and guilt. The role that shame plays in restorative processes has become increasingly discussed and theorised since the early 1990s. This was initially in relation to offenders: the argument being that offenders should be 'shamed' within a supportive and loving continuum, so that they would appreciate the seriousness of what they had done but still be valued as a person (Braithwaite 1989; Braithwaite and Mugford 1994). However, observations of conferences has led to a much wider recognition of the role played by shame (Moore and Forsythe 1995; Retzinger and Scheff 1996). Some now consider conferences to be a process through which all present move through various emotional states. For example, McDonald and Moore (2001: 138) argue that:

> the crucial dynamic is not that *one* conference participant expresses shame, and thereby clears the hurdle beyond which reintegration can occur. Rather, the crucial dynamic is that *all participants* experience a sense of shame, and this experience marks the transition from a generally negative emotional climate to a generally positive emotional climate. The collective experience of shame marks the transition from conflict to cooperation.

For McDonald and Moore (2001: 139), a conference is 'a mechanism by which the negative emotions associated with conflict can be transformed into the positive emotions associated with cooperation'. This draws on the work of shame theorists such as Nathanson (1992), Retzinger (1991) and Scheff (1994), among whom there is broad consistency. In short, all of these theorists argue that shame is a much misunderstood emotion, present in every social situation, able to dramatically influence both feelings and behaviour. They argue that any upset to how people expect the world to be, or would like the world to be, causes a threat to individual identity and their relationships with others. People experience varying levels of shame when things do not go as planned, with shame serving to tell us that something is awry. Shame is an important regulator of social life and social bonds. When conflicts arise with others, when people feel slighted or disrespected in some way, they experience feelings of hurt and shame. This will often be expressed as anger and aggression, but they are ultimately motivated by underlying feelings of shame and hurt. Nathanson (1992) considers that each experience of shame reminds us of previous shame experiences, and that we develop 'scripts' that determine our likely response to being in a state of shame. The most common four reactions are to attack the self, attack others, avoid the issue pretending it has not occurred, or withdraw as a person.

Nathanson argues that in a minority of circumstances people react by accepting the situation, learning from it and changing. This is perhaps akin to the final stage of the crisis reaction: negative feelings are acknowledged, 'mourned' (Herman 1992) and eventually dissipate as people integrate their experiences and develop a new sense of self.

Retzinger and Scheff, from their observations of conferences, consider that 'awareness and negotiation of shame dynamics are the keys to effective conferences'. They argue that a two-stage 'core sequence' is necessary for the successful resolution of a conference, and for the reduction of tension: 'the offender first clearly expresses genuine shame and remorse over his or her actions. In response, the victim takes at least a first step towards forgiving the offender for the trespass' (1996: 316).

Without any obvious reference to the literature on how people react to victimisation, Retzinger and Scheff (1996: 322) identify that victims are 'likely to feel the shame of helplessness, impotence, betrayal, and/or violation', though these feelings are often 'masked' by anger and indignation. In common to Herman's model, uncovering and acknowledging such hidden emotions of shame, hurt, fear and grief appears central to enabling victims to escape these feelings. Common mediation practice is to have victims tell their stories and identify their emotions prior to meeting the offender. This enables victims to clarify what it may be they wish to say in the actual meeting. A fairly frequent occurrence in practice though, is that having had this preparation meeting with the mediators, many victims feel that they have recovered enough not to need the actual meeting. It has yet to be established if 'telling their story' to the offender is more effective then relating it to a mediator, and there are many examples from practice of how interaction with a mediator alone has greatly helped victim recovery. In this form, mediation practice may be very similar to counselling methods, and is certainly similar to the methods advocated by Herman (1992) in relation to PTSD.

The role of forgiveness

Some victims do wish to forgive their offenders, often because of their own religious or moral beliefs (see Dickey 1998 for examples). While it has yet to be established empirically how important forgiveness is for victims in general, there is little qualitative evidence that this explicitly matters to a majority of victims. My own practice experience supports this. Victims want to know what is happening with the case, and they are generally interested in finding out, sometimes in person, if the offender is remorseful or not – this is important to many victims. This has struck me as representing a desire to know that the offender recognises their culpability, perhaps representing some capacity to care about the feelings of others on the part of the offender. Victims are particularly interested to find out what the court sentence received by the offender will actually mean in practice. Perhaps surprisingly to some readers, most victims do *not* wish the offender to be harshly punished, and are impressed to hear that most young offenders (in England and Wales) are required to do some form of 'reparation work', making a positive contribution to the community in some way.

Most victims are also interested in knowing a little about the offender, what they currently do in life and what their aspirations are etc. Victims seem to wish to know that the offender is normal, not abnormal. Victims are almost all pleased to know that offenders do often receive quite considerable support aimed at preventing further offending. For many victims, finding out that someone, somewhere, is taking what has happened seriously and doing something, appears to be very satisfying. In my experience, it is only a very small minority of victims who explicitly talk about wishing to forgive the offender(s).

Indeed, practitioners are explicitly advised against suggesting forgiveness as a potential motivation or outcome. One training manual provides the following reasons for this, with which I strongly concur.

> It is important that mediators avoid the use of words such as 'forgiveness' or 'reconciliation' – such words pressure and prescribe behavior for victims. Some victims may experience something of reconciliation, but it must occur spontaneously, without a directive from the mediator. In fact, it is more likely to occur if the mediator avoids directives. Forgiveness also may be expressed during the mediation session but if the mediator so much as uses the word 'forgiveness' it may be destructive to the victim. Victims may, for instance, feel guilty if they fail to feel very forgiving. They may resent the suggestion and shut down to the point that they miss the opportunity to truly express how the crime has impacted them, typically a healing piece in a victim's journey.
>
> (Umbreit and Greenwood 1998)

Herman (1992: 189), in her discussion of the importance of people 'remembering and mourning' traumatic events, considers that 'some survivors attempt to bypass their outrage altogether through a fantasy of forgiveness – the survivor imagines that she can transcend her rage and erase the impact of the trauma through a willed, defiant, act of love'. Somewhat echoing the advice of Umbreit and Greenwood (1998) above, Herman (1992: 190) considers that 'It is not possible to exorcise the trauma, through either hatred or love. Like revenge, the fantasy of forgiveness often becomes a cruel torture, because it remains out of reach for most ordinary human beings'. She believes that 'true forgiveness cannot be granted until the perpetrator has sought and earned it through confession, repentance and restitution'. This is akin to the 'core sequence' argued as necessary for effective conferences by Retzinger and Scheff (1996).

Forgiveness therapy

Recently, Enright and colleagues (Enright and North 1998; Enright and Fitzgibbons 2000) have argued that 'helping clients forgive', following traumatic events, can be a powerful and successful intervention. Enright and Fitzgibbons (2000: 23–4) that:

Forgiveness has a specific task: to help people overcome resentment, bitterness, and even hatred toward people who have treated them unfairly and at times cruelly – forgiveness is a specialist in quelling that kind of anger that debilitates the injured or wounded individual . . . through the process of working at forgiving and compassionately understanding offenders, clients will become freed from the negative or toxic effects of their own justifiable anger.

Enright and Fitzgibbons describe a four-stage 'phase model of the forgiveness process'. In the first 'uncovering phase', the client must understand that they have been harmed or treated unjustly in some way, and this has hurt them. Feelings of anger arising from this hurt need to be acknowledged, as well as feelings of shame and resentment against those responsible. Also in this phase, the client must 'face the fact that the unfairness has changed his or her life', and perhaps brought about doubt that the world is just. It is clear that there are strong similarities with the processes advocated by Bard and Sangrey (1986) and Herman (1992). Significant differences emerge in the second 'decision phase', however. In this phase the clients are asked to consider if forgiveness might be a method through which they can relieve themselves of feelings of resentment. Enright and Fitzgibbons (2000: 24) thoroughly acknowledge that this is a cognitive decision based in morality. Forgiving is defined as:

> People, upon rationally determining that they have been unfairly treated, forgive when they willfully abandon resentment and related responses (to which they have a right), and endeavour to respond to the wrongdoer based on the moral principle of beneficence, which may include compassion, unconditional worth, generosity, and moral love (to which the wrongdoer, by nature of the hurtful act or acts, has no right).

If they decide to pursue forgiveness, clients enter into the third 'work phase', regarded as 'the deep process of forgiveness'. They are asked a series of questions to challenge their views of the offender, and to begin to see them as a fellow human being worthy of compassion, rather than 'evil incarnate'. Clients are asked to consider what it may have been like for the offender when they were growing up, at the time of the offence, and whether the client can recognise them 'as a member of the human community'. Following this, it should be possible for the client to feel empathy and compassion for the offender. Forgiveness should then be possible and recognised as the moral gift that it is (within this model). In the final 'deepening phase', clients are encouraged to create new meanings from their suffering, consider how relief from suffering can be achieved, how others may benefit from changes in the client's views and behaviour, and the place of suffering in the world. Clients consider the moments in their life when they may have needed the forgiveness of others, and what this meant for them. Many clients go on to realise a 'new purpose', motivated by their experiences.

Enright and Fitzgibbons (2000) offer a wide range of empirical data validating this model as useful to people suffering from trauma brought about by a range of events, including victims of serious crimes. There is much commonality between the cognitive forgiveness model and the emotional models underpinning restorative practice, particularly that negative feelings are caused by unacknowledged feelings of hurt and shame. It is significant that the 'solution' to this is also common among all of the models discussed in this chapter: the need to tell their 'trauma' story, to give 'testimony' (Zehr 2000), focusing on the underlying feelings of hurt, fear, grief and shame. The most significant difference is whether forgiveness should be an unmentioned result through interaction, or explicitly sought from the outset with the full knowledge of the victim.

Concluding words – can forgiveness therapy and restorative justice be reconciled?

It is clear that this developing forgiveness field should remain of key interest to those interested in restorative justice, as well as those working in the psychotherapeutic field with individuals. Forgiveness therapy may well lead to the revision of some of the core views that I have expressed in this chapter and significant changes in practice. Most notably, it could lead to the suggestion being made to some victims that they should decide to forgive, and work toward forgiving those who harmed them. I believe that many restorative justice practitioners would find such a change difficult to consider. However, it should also be remembered that it has been very difficult for many experienced in the criminal justice field to accept that victims and offenders can meet and discuss, civilly, the offence. Revolutions, however small, do happen. My own perspective is that restorative justice practitioners should consider pursuing forgiveness therapy with victims who still present as traumatised following the conclusion of established restorative practice.

However, there is no doubt that the term 'forgiveness' will remain a controversial issue for many victims of crime, as demonstrated by the following comment from a victim of sexual abuse, reported by Yantzi (1998: 124): 'It would be most helpful if we could get rid of the word forgiveness and create a fresh, new term to capture what is meant'. Until this new term is, if ever, found, Yantzi (1998: 134) perhaps best captures the views of many, that 'forgiveness is best understood, not as a process with specific steps, but rather [as something that victims] look back on later and say, "Yes, healing happened". Some people may label that forgiveness'. From a restorative justice perspective, the key is that criminal justice systems should investigate and provide every possible intervention known to be effective in assisting victim recovery.

References

Bard, M. and Sangrey, D. (1986) *The Crime Victim's Book*, 2nd edn. New York: Brunner/Mazel.

Bazemore, G. and Walgrave, L. (2000) Restorative juvenile justice: in search of fundamentals and an outline for systemic reform, in G. Bazemore and L. Walgrave (eds) *Restorative Juvenile Justice: Repairing the Harm of Youth Crime*. Monsey, New York: Criminal Justice Press.

Braithwaite, J. (1989) *Crime, Shame and Reintegration*. Cambridge: Cambridge University Press.

Braithwaite, J. and Mugford, S. (1994) Conditions of successful reintegration ceremonies: dealing with juvenile offenders, *British Journal of Criminology*, 34(2): 139–71.

Coates, R. and Gehm, J. (1989) An empirical assessment, in M. Wright and B. Galaway (eds) *Mediation and Criminal Justice*. London: Sage.

Daly, K. (2000) Restorative justice: the real story. Paper presented at the Scottish Criminology Conference, Edinburgh, 21–2 September.

Daly, K. (2002) Mind the gap: restorative justice in theory and practice, in A. von Hirsch, J. Roberts, A.E. Bottoms, K. Roach and M. Schiff (eds) *Restorative Justice and Criminal Justice: Competing or Reconcilable Paradigms?* Oxford: Hart Publishing.

Davis, G. (1992) *Making Amends: Mediation and Reparation in Criminal Justice*. London: Routledge.

Dickey, W. (1998) Forgiveness and crime: the possibilities of restorative justice, in R. Enright and J. North (eds) *Exploring Forgiveness*. Madison, WI: University of Wisconsin Press.

Enright, R. and North, J. (eds) (1998) *Exploring Forgiveness*. Madison, WI: University of Wisconsin Press.

Enright, R. and Fitzgibbons, R. (2000) *Helping Clients Forgive: An Empirical Guide for Resolving Anger and Restoring Hope*. Washington: American Psychological Association.

Giuliano, B. (1998) *Survival and Beyond: An Anthology of Stories by Victims of Crime, and a Victims' Resource Guide*. Australian Capital Territory: The National Association for Loss and Grief.

Herman, J. (1992) *Trauma and Recovery*. New York: Basic Books.

McDonald, J. and Moore, D. (2001) Community conferencing as a special case of conflict transformation, in H. Strang and J. Braithwaite (eds) *Restorative Justice and Civil Society*. Cambridge: Cambridge University Press.

Maguire, M. and Corbett, C. (1987) *The Effects of Crime and the Work of Victims Support Schemes*. Aldershot: Gower.

Marshall, T. and Merry, S. (1990) *Crime and Accountability*. London: Home Office.

Masters, G. (2001) The boldest initiative for victims? Reviewing the limits and potential of restorative justice for victims of crime. Paper presented at the 5th International Conference on Restorative Justice for Juveniles, Leuven, September.

Mawby, R. and Walklate, S. (1994) *Critical Victimology: International Perspectives*. London: Sage.

Maxwell, G. and Morris, A. (1993) *Family, Victims and Culture: Youth Justice in New Zealand*. Wellington: Social Policy Agency and Institute of Criminology, Victoria University of Wellington.

Mediation UK (1994) *Victim-Offender Mediation Conference 9th February 1994* (collected papers). Bristol: Mediation UK.

Mediation UK (2001) *The Rough Guide to Restorative Justice and the Crime and Disorder Act*. Bristol: Mediation UK.

Mollica, R. (1988) The trauma story: the psychiatric care of refugee survivors of violence and torture, in F. Ochberg (ed.) *Post-Traumatic Therapy and Victims of Violence*. New York: Brunner/Mazel.

Moore, D. and Forsythe, L. (1995) *A New Approach to Juvenile Justice: An Evaluation of Family Conferencing in Wagga Wagga*. New South Wales: Charles Sturt University.

Nathanson, D. (1992) *Shame and Pride: Affect, Sex and the Birth of the Self*. London: Norton.

Peachey, D. (1989) The Kitchener experiment, in M. Wright and B. Galaway (eds) *Mediation and Criminal Justice*. London: Sage.

Retzinger, S. (1991) *Violent Emotions: Shame and Rage in Marital Quarrels*. Newbury Park, CA: Sage.

Retzinger, S. and Scheff, T. (1996) Strategy for community conferences: emotions and social bonds, in B. Galaway and J. Hudson (eds) *Restorative Justice: International Perspectives*. New York: Criminal Justice Press.

Scheff, T. (1994) *Bloody Revenge. Emotions, Nationalism and War*. Oxford: Westview Press.

Shapland J., Willmore, J. and Duff, P. (1985) *Victims in the Criminal Justice System*. Aldershot: Gower.

Strang, H. (2000) Victim participation in a restorative justice process: the Canberra Reintegrative Shaming Experiments. Phd thesis, Centre for Restorative Justice, Australian National University.

Strang, H. and Sherman, L. (1997) *RISE Working Papers: Paper No. 2 The Victim's Perspective*. Canberra: Australian National University.

Umbreit, M. (1989) Violent offenders and their victims, in M. Wright and B. Galaway (eds) *Mediation and Criminal Justice*. London: Sage.

Umbreit, M. (1994) *Victim Meets Offender: The Impact of Restorative Justice and Mediation*. Monsey, New York: Criminal Justice Press.

Umbreit, M. (ed.) (1998) *Victim Sensitive Victim Offender Mediation Training Manual*. St Paul, MN: Center for Restorative Justice and Peacemaking, University of Minnesota.

Umbreit, M. and Greenwood, J. (1998) Guidelines for victim sensitive mediation and dialogue with offenders, in M. Umbreit (ed.) *Victim Sensitive Victim Offender Mediation Training Manual*. St Paul, MN: Center for Restorative Justice and Peacemaking, University of Minnesota.

Umbreit, M. and Roberts, A. (1996) *Mediation of Criminal Conflict in England: An Assessment of Services in Coventry and Leeds*. St Paul, MN: Center for Restorative Justice and Peacemaking, University of Minnesota.

Wright, M. (1996) *Justice for Victims and Offenders*, 2nd edn. Winchester: Waterside Press.

Yantzi, M. (1998) *Sexual Offending and Restoration*. Ontario: Herald Press.

Zehr, H. (1990) *Changing Lenses*. Ontario: Herald Press.

Zehr, H. (2000) Journey to Belonging. Paper presented to the 4th International Conference on Restorative Justice for Juveniles, Tübingen, Germany, 1–4 October 2000.

Chapter 7

In the aftermath of political trauma: what price forgiveness?

Fathima Moosa, Gill Straker and Gill Eagle

Introduction

It is our basic premise that forgiveness is a desirable objective for individuals, as it acts as a catalyst for peace, both personal and interpersonal. It is also our belief that this is not an absolute, and that when individuals or groups find, in good faith, that they are unable to forgive those who have wronged them, their choice not to forgive is no less worthy of respect. For when forgiveness, like peace, is adopted as a line of least resistance, there is premature foreclosure on challenging situations which, if confronted openly and honestly, could serve as a spur to further growth. Our view is based on a recognition of the special complexities of the question of forgiveness in contexts of political trauma.

As our reflections are informed by our work with victims of apartheid-induced trauma and its aftermath, our discussion of forgiveness in relation to political trauma will be based on experiences derived from the South African context. Our observations are informed by the therapeutic work we have engaged in with victims of political violence over approximately two decades. It is also derived from our discussions with four colleagues who have been similarly involved in offering counselling services to victims of political trauma in South Africa. In addition, our conclusions are based on an analysis of the work of South Africa's Truth and Reconciliation Commission (TRC). Given the centrality of reconciliation to its functioning, the TRC has become emblematic of the struggles with forgiveness experienced by victims of political trauma. It is germane to present a brief outline of the TRC before proceeding with our analysis of the complexities of forgiveness in contexts of political trauma which it highlighted.

The Truth and Reconciliation Commission (TRC)

The TRC in South Africa was set up in order to address the issue of human rights violations that had been perpetrated during the years of apartheid rule. It was a compromise between the former apartheid government's push for a blanket amnesty for its members and agents on the one hand, and the pressure for Nuremberg-type trials advocated by some among the ranks of the liberation movements on the other.

A blanket amnesty was opposed as it appeared to dismiss the injuries and trauma to which victims had been exposed. Conversely, the call for punitive Nuremberg-type trials was rejected as potentially very divisive and likely to foment further conflict in an already deeply divided society. It was also seen as reducing the possibility of negotiating a settlement in which the apartheid government would begin the process of relinquishing power. Thus, the TRC was established in 1995 to encourage those responsible for committing human rights violations to disclose their deeds in a public forum, and to enable their former victims to hear these confessions. In addition, victims were invited to 'tell their stories' so that their suffering could be acknowledged by the community at large and they could receive the support to which they were entitled. The objective was to restore to them the dignity that their former oppressors had attempted to strip from them. In order to achieve its objectives, the TRC's task was to juggle amnesty for the perpetrators with reparations for the victims. In exchange for perpetrators' full disclosure of the politically motivated atrocities in which they had engaged, they would be granted amnesty against prosecution. The victims, in turn, were encouraged to reconcile themselves to this process, while instances of victims' explicit forgiveness of perpetrators were especially affirmed.

Thus, the injunction to forgive was implicit in the functioning of the TRC, as its major concern was to facilitate peaceful coexistence between the perpetrators of extreme and traumatic human rights violations and the victims on whom these had been inflicted.

The TRC consisted of three committees: the Committee on Human Rights Violations, the Amnesty Committee, and the Committee for Reparation and Rehabilitation. The Committee on Human Rights Violations was entrusted with inviting and hearing the testimony of victims. The task of the Amnesty Committee was to hear and investigate the submissions of perpetrators, while the brief of the Committee for Reparation and Rehabilitation was to offer some form of reparation, symbolic and/or material, to address the injustices that had occurred.

The degree of success the TRC attained is the subject of much debate (Hamber and Wilson 1999; Mamdani 2001), but this will not specifically be considered here. Instead, our focus will essentially be on the aspect of forgiveness – i.e. on the work of the TRC as an institution and the representations of victims to it, where these pertain to the issue of forgiveness. In particular, our concern is with the way the TRC, in seeking to promote reconciliation, may have prejudged the role of forgiveness in creating healing and resolution for victims. We would argue that, while it was undoubtedly well intentioned in its purpose and *modus operandi*, it may have undermined its own efforts and perhaps rendered itself somewhat ineffectual by insufficiently addressing the profound complexity of the notion and experience of forgiveness.

The complexity of forgiveness in contexts of political trauma

A psychological understanding of the intrapsychic and interpersonal process of forgiveness is still relatively undeveloped (Fow 1996; Sells and Hargrave 1998; Doyle 1999). The inherently complicated nature of forgiveness is emphasised by writers who define it as 'paradoxical'. For example, Freedman and Enright (1996: 983) observe that 'There is a decided paradoxical quality to forgiveness as the forgiver gives up the resentment, to which he or she has a right, and gives the gift of compassion, to which the offender has no right'. However, the burden of forgiveness is particularly complex in relation to contexts of political trauma. Forgiveness in a broader political context differs from its manifestation in narrower (inter)personal situations, along several dimensions. The ideas formulated in work with individuals cannot simply be extrapolated to those involved in political struggles, as the observations made inevitably have implications of a broader political nature. When the issue arises in a politically loaded setting, the individual's response is necessarily more complicated. As this discussion hopes to show, the choice regarding whether, or how much, to forgive has wider implications beyond the individual.

While forgiveness in interpersonal situations (e.g. in instances where individuals have been abused) does have a political dimension, as exemplified in the feminist rallying cry of 'the personal is political', the choice to forgive has an extra dimension in contexts of political trauma. Forgiveness in these situations is often not experienced as a personal choice only, but one that has implications for other people. Thus, for political activists, the choice of whether to forgive or not represents a political position.

This was exemplified, for example, by the dilemma of individuals who had been involved in conflicts that had torn communities apart in some townships in South Africa during the 1980s and early 1990s. As a result, internal conflict within communities became rife. During the ensuing battles, many individuals were dispossessed, injured or killed. Following the efforts by the government of Nelson Mandela to end the violence in the country at large and the townships in particular, individuals were faced with the challenge of coexisting peacefully with their former enemies. They were encouraged to forgive their enemies (including those that had been in collusion with the apartheid forces). It was argued that the reconstruction of a new society, free of the infighting and violence that had characterised the preceding decades, required reconciliation between former foes. Apart from the inherent personal challenges that forgiveness entails, the considerable reluctance of many to offer such forgiveness was informed by their fear that they would lose their hard-won political power. The choice to forgive or not had a political currency, so that forgiveness functioned almost like a commodity; thus, conferring forgiveness was experienced as generating political advantage or disadvantage for the individual.

The degree to which individuals may feel caught between their personal feelings and their political loyalties is reflected in the interesting (if unwitting) distinction between forgiveness and reconciliation made by some political activists. Reconciling with former enemies with whom they had to attempt to coexist in a post-liberation South Africa was considered a strategic necessity, even though an internal forgiveness was considered too difficult if not impossible to attain.

Hence the concepts of forgiveness and reconciliation as understood by these individuals contrasts markedly with the way they are defined in the theoretical literature. For instance, Freedman and Enright (1996) argue that while it is necessary for the psychological well-being of individuals to forgive those who inflicted traumatic experiences on them, this does not necessarily require a reconciliation with the perpetrator. This view is also advanced by therapists who work with victims of sexual abuse. Thus, the change advocated is primarily an internal rather than an external one. The stance of some of the individuals with whom we worked, in contrast, was that in the interests of community harmony and national reconciliation (and because the cause for which they had fought required it of them), they were prepared to bracket their inner feelings of non-forgiveness and to reconcile with the perpetrator in the external world.

It is essential that therapists are cognisant of these wider ramifications of an individual's decision to forgive. The offering of forgiveness may be perceived as having positive consequences (e.g. in the gaining of political advantage when the individual's stance, whether one of forgiveness or non-forgiveness, is in accord with the official position of the political movement to which she or he belongs). Conversely, in adopting a position that is at odds with that of the political movement to which the individual belongs, she or he may risk being marginalised.

The recognition by the therapist of this quandary is important. It is necessary to explore the extent to which politically involved individuals feel that they are not choosing for themselves alone. Since allegiance to one's comrades is a central guiding principle for political activists, it is an imperative for them that they do not break ranks. Similarly, adhering to the principles defining their common cause is a central creed for politically committed individuals. Consequently, for these individuals, opting to forgive or not, when their personal inclinations contradict the policy of the movement to which they belong, may lead them to experience a profound sense of conflict. Thus, they may feel that they are acting or behaving in a way that is a betrayal of all they hold dear – and thus could be a form of further trauma for them.

Hence, in working with individuals for whom their identity as political activists has been central, therapists would need to facilitate a fuller exploration of the meaning and wider political implications for them of their choices regarding forgiveness. Not to do so would risk engendering further traumatic consequences for the individual through well-meaning but naïve interventions. If, on the other hand, individuals are able to work through their options fully, they will be better prepared to confront the consequences of their choices, and to possibly minimise potential negative consequences for themselves. By examining the personal and political implications of their decisions regarding forgiveness in a safe therapeutic space, the feelings (e.g. of ambivalence and confusion) attendant on this process may be contained. This would allow them to be better prepared for the consequences they are likely to encounter. Consequently, their decisions would be more likely to be made from a position of strength within themselves, and would not simply emanate from internal and/or external pressures. This process is important as action without prior reflection may generate further difficulties for the individual.

In considering the question of forgiveness, it is not only the individual's political affiliation but also the community with which she or he identifies that is a further, or alternative, point of reference. Individuals have sometimes reflected on how difficult it is to make a personal decision about forgiveness when the atmosphere within the community is strongly for, or against, it. Instances were encountered, for example, when the prevailing mood in the community made it seem impossible for individuals to forgive, even if they preferred to do so. Thus, individuals expressed a personal inclination to forgive particular people (e.g. former neighbours who might have been regarded as informers), but felt unable to do so lest they court the community's disfavour. This dilemma was especially evident during the height of the conflict between the African National Congress (ANC) and Inkatha in KwaZulu-Natal in the period preceding and following the elections that brought the ANC to power in South Africa. The political rivalry between the two groups was intense and feelings ran deep, so that any act of violence was seen as requiring retaliation. In this situation, individuals who privately expressed a wish to forgive the perpetrators who may have injured them or someone close to them felt unable to do so.

Therapists working with these individuals found that their approaches required modification in terms of the context within which they were working. Thus, in contexts of ongoing political violence, supporting the individual's need to forgive in the face of the risk of ostracism by his or her comrades posed a challenge. Some therapists attempted to meet this challenge by distinguishing between a private (or personal) mode of forgiveness and its interpersonal, shared expression. It was suggested that since it was unrealistic in the circumstances to offer forgiveness, this could be seen as a deferred form of forgiveness which could be expressed when appropriate.

Vicarious forgiveness

It is noteworthy that while individuals experienced some tension in deciding whether to forgive perpetrators who had harmed them personally, their dilemma was compounded when their choice whether to forgive was taken on behalf of another. This often involved some reference to community expectations and cultural beliefs. The observation by some political activists (even when the political tensions had abated) that it would be difficult to offer forgiveness owing to the cultural belief system to which they subscribed, is a reflection of this. In particular, they alluded to cultural norms that they believed require retribution in order to right major wrongs. They observed that, within their cultural framework, the family is responsible, in a literal way, to the dead person's spirit; it was believed that the spirit would not rest without revenge (and not just symbolic revenge). Thus, some ambivalence was expressed about the prospect that, in the course of uncovering the truth, the TRC would reveal the identity of those responsible for the deaths of some of their family members. Some political activists noted that, paradoxically, an ignorance of the killers' identity allowed them to support the TRC's doctrine of forgiveness and reconciliation in abstract terms. However, they felt that once the identities of the perpetrators was revealed, it was incumbent on them to observe the customs of their culture which, they believed, necessitated the exacting of vengeance. This was an interesting subverting of the TRC's doctrine of 'Truth: the road to reconciliation'.

Therapists encountering this somewhat more idiosyncratic rebuttal of the TRC's, and indeed their own, view that the process of healing was necessarily contingent on the articulation of the truth, were once again reminded of the complicated nature of facilitating forgiveness in contexts of political trauma. In addressing this dilemma, it is necessary to implement an intervention that is multi-faceted. Thus, it would be appropriate to intervene at the level of involving community leaders who have credibility with the individuals, and who are able to address their concerns regarding the apparent failure to avenge their family members. Alternative cultural rituals may be followed in order to appease the souls of the dead victims. Through these means, individuals are enabled to give expression to their need to forgive, without feelings of guilt about failing to exact vengeance.

The interventions suggested are concerned with addressing cultural beliefs and perceived community expectations. However, it may also be useful to consider the intrapsychic processes that may operate when individuals confront the question of whether to forgive on behalf of a family member who was killed, disabled or disappeared. For them, part of their difficulty with forgiveness may be related to feelings of guilt at having been unable to protect their loved ones from harm. Thus, they might experience the notion of forgiving the perpetrator as another betrayal or dereliction of duty. The example of the Argentinian mothers of the disappeared who refused to compromise on the return of their loved ones as a condition of dialogue, despite the impossibility of this, may be seen as an illustration. Thus, the issue of whether some form of revenge is beholden on those who survive the deceased begs the question of whether forgiveness or retaliation is the preferred form of memorial.

In considering the difficulties of forgiving on behalf of another, it would also be important to analyse the state's or community's role in this regard. As the foregoing discussion suggests, the question of who is entitled to confer forgiveness is not necessarily clear cut. Since the individual is accountable to the community, which also carries the sense of injury when one of its members is wronged, forgiveness is not necessarily seen as an individual decision only. However, the establishment of the TRC raised the question of whether the state is also entitled to forgive the perpetrator (i.e. in the form of amnesty) on the victim's behalf. This was noted by Straker (2001), who observed:

> It should be noted that in guiding beneficiaries and perpetrators to liberation through acknowledgment of shame and disgust it was the TRC itself which dispensed forgiveness, not the direct victims of the events in question.
>
> That this was the case was crucial for the mental health of all concerned, for forgiveness can never legitimately be asked for from the victim. This is an unfair burden to place on the shoulders of those who are already deeply injured. In fact one of the criticisms of the TRC and the culture that it promoted, was that it inadvertently placed pressure on the already traumatised to transcend their situation in particular ways and it

tended to make those who did not wish to take this route feel guilty.

The aspect that most clearly distinguishes forgiveness in inter-personal contexts and forgiveness in contexts of political trauma is that of choice. For in cases of political trauma, not only is the choice whether to forgive imbued with profound political implica-tions which extend beyond the individual, but the very decision regarding the choice to forgive may be seemingly appropriated by institutions which were intended to represent one's interests (e.g. the TRC). The TRC's power to grant amnesty to perpetrators was sometimes viewed as a denial of the victim's right to withhold forgiveness. This was especially ironic given that one of the features of trauma is the imposition of the perpetrator's will on the victim.

However, it must be acknowledged that the undertaking of the TRC was a profoundly challenging one. In being vested with the power to grant amnesty to perpetrators, it was in effect pardoning them for their actions and implicitly allowing them to shed the burden of culpability for the traumas they had inflicted. Although a legal pardon does not necessarily confer moral absolution, the role of the TRC has been seen, to some extent, as one of forgiving and thus apparently absolving perpetrators on the victims' behalf. This perception has perhaps been lent credence by the conduct of the TRC itself, given its clearly sympathetic stance towards and (implicit identification with) victims (Tutu 1999). It is therefore ironic that it has been criticised for failing victims and instead furthering the interests of perpetrators. However, as the relative success of the TRC in meeting its own objectives is outside the scope of this chapter, this will not be examined in detail.

Perhaps a resolution of the question whether the state, through the establishment of the TRC, has a right to forgive on behalf of the victim, or is usurping this right, lies in the aspect of redress. As previously discussed, forgiveness may be viewed in social terms, in which individuals' choice or scope to forgive may be mediated by their political group or community.

Reparations

A related aspect influencing individuals' capacity to forgive is, in large measure, that of their current life circumstances. As this clearly signifies, the capacity to forgive is not only internally determined, but to some extent, also externally informed. Thus, a willingness to forgive is also based on factors such as individuals' material conditions, social standing and their related sense of efficacy in the world.

This has obvious implications for the question of reparations, as the capacity to forgive is fostered by the provision of redress which is of sufficient magnitude to allow individuals to feel that they are no longer carrying the damage of the trauma in a current sense, but only in a historical one. Hence, reparations need to be meaningful rather than being experienced as token, since the perception of fairness in relation to individuals' experience of trauma fosters their ability to forgive.

In South Africa, it was part of the brief of the TRC to recommend appropriate reparations for victims of politically related trauma. However, the issue of reparations has become a contentious issue for the TRC as its efforts in this area have been a source of frustration both for its own members (Orr 2000) and for the victims of human rights violations who testified before it. These victims had regarded the TRC as a broker between themselves and the government which had attained power largely on the basis of the traumatic sacrifices they had made. The apparent failure of this new government (which was constituted by many former comrades of victims seeking redress through the TRC) to deliver on the aspect of reparations, profoundly complicated the work of forgiveness for these victims.

This was noted by Chubb and Van Dijk (2001: 213), who observed that:

> There is clearly a rising tide of anger and disillusionment among those who testified before the TRC. While the opportunity to tell one's story and have one's suffering acknowledged is indeed a form of reparation, it cannot remain the only one. The government's apparent refusal to honour its commitments on reparations is inflicting more injuries on those who have already suffered, ironically in the general cause of putting this very government into power.

This conclusion is borne out by the experiences of therapists engaged in counselling victims of politically related trauma. For instance, an example (which is prototypical) was cited of an individual, formerly employed as a professional, who subsequently lost his position and suffered many years of unemployment following imprisonment for his political involvement. His attempts to work through his traumatic experiences were undermined by the profound sense of frustration he felt at receiving no recompense for all he had lost in terms of his career. In particular, his anger was fuelled by the contrast between his ongoing material difficulties and his perception of his former comrades as having attained success in the corporate and/or political spheres. Thus, the apparent reluctance of the ANC government to implement the TRC's recommendations regarding substantial reparations for individuals such as himself provoked a sense of being betrayed. When most assailed by these internal conflicts, he was moved to observe that sometimes he could forgive his former enemies more easily than his former comrades who, having attained personal and professional success appeared to have forgotten those who had also contributed to the overthrow of apartheid at great personal cost. As this example clearly indicates, harsh material conditions exacerbate feelings of anger and bitterness and undermine the capacity to forgive.

The suggestion that victims may experience forgiveness as an emotional luxury which those struggling with the exigencies of everyday survival can ill afford, is also contained in the observation by Chubb and Van Dijk (2001: 3) that: 'many experience the idea of reconciliation as something reserved for those "who can afford it" as one youth mentioned at a hearing'.

While the perceived discrepancy in material circumstances and social mobility between individuals within the liberation movements was identified as a source of frustration for some, the overwhelming majority of victims expressed anger at the continued imbalance between their lot and that of their former oppressors. Many victims expressed the feeling that those who obtained amnesty had received a better deal. The perception of inequities in reparation vs. amnesty contributed to a perpetuation of a sense of injustice for the victims. The sentiment was expressed that they would not have accepted the idea of the TRC if they had known that it would be so easy for the perpetrators to be absolved of their guilt, and that the victims would have so little sense of redress.

The victim's capacity to forgive in these circumstances is influenced by several considerations. The foremost of these appears to be the degree to which the perpetrators may have benefited from (or are perceived to be enjoying) a lifestyle of affluence or greater comfort than the victims. While on a personal level, the injustice this represents for victims may be a source of frustration, the perceived differential has larger implications for victims. Thus, for example, disquiet is expressed by victims who reflect that not only do their erstwhile oppressors continue to function (e.g. as policemen), but in some instances, may even have been promoted subsequently to more senior positions.

The moral dilemma of granting amnesty to perpetrators, without a guarantee of equivalent redress to victims, is captured in the analogy offered by Laurie Nathan:

> Look at it this way: I steal your bicycle. After five years I come to you and say, 'I am very sorry, I stole your bicycle.' You may, if you are Archbishop Tutu, say, 'I forgive you.' The more normal response would be, 'Yes, okay – where is my bicycle?' If what I stole was not your bicycle but your land, your dreams, your hope? What then? How much does my apology count?
>
> (Chubb and Van Dijk 2001: 181)

Given that one of the motivations underlying the popular insurrection in South Africa was a need to redistribute material resources, the apparently ongoing greater access to such resources by the former perpetrator/beneficiary represents a perceived failure of the 'armed struggle' to deliver. It is therefore not surprising that victims, in reflecting on the degree to which they have compromised on their former expectations, expressed doubts regarding the extent to which their contributions had made a difference. The relatively greater benefits apparently enjoyed by the perpetrator left them questioning the meaning of the sacrifices they had made and the suffering they had endured. Thus, the reluctance of victims to forgive in these circumstances is expressive of a dilemma that does not simply pertain to their own situation. Their resistance to forgiving perpetrators who continue to enjoy what they consider to be ill-gotten gains is a communication that they refuse to confer a tacit approval to a dispensation which not only fails to acknowledge their considerable losses, but seemingly rewards their oppressors by failing to call them to account in a significant way. Thus, the TRC process may ultimately have left some victims, at best, struggling with the meaning of their suffering, or at worst, feeling that the trauma they experienced was endured in vain and that the cause for which they struggled was a futile one. That TRC members were cognisant of this difficulty is evident in the observation by Chubb and Van Dijk (2001: 212) that: 'The continuing credibility and moral force of the TRC rests on a crucial balance between amnesty and reparations'. Thus, it is essential that reparations and retribution/punishment are perceived to be fair and just, to facilitate a capacity to forgive.

Forgiveness: further catalysts and impediments

Exposure of the perpetrator's fallibility and flaws

Counter-arguments to the perception that perpetrators received amnesty while remaining unaccountable have been advanced. For example, Tutu emphasised that:

> The applicant must therefore make his admissions in the full glare of publicity. Let us imagine what this means. Often this is the first time that an applicant's family and community learn that an apparently decent man was, for instance, a callous torturer or a member of a ruthless death squad that assassinated many opponents of the previous regime. There is, therefore, a price to be paid. Public disclosure results in public shaming.
>
> (Chubb and Van Dijk 2001: 227)

Other commentators on the work of the TRC have noted the powerful effect of seeing individuals who would previously have been able to wield arbitrary and seemingly total power over victims, humbled before their former victims. Thus, for instance, being able to see the security policeman, Benzien, who had been guilty of many acts of torture being compelled to demonstrate, on his knees, the experiences some torture victims had endured at his hands was a dramatic illustration of his current powerlessness (Orr 2000). Although the objective was not one of deliberately subjecting him to indignity, this was an incidental consequence of his amnesty application and appearance before the TRC. Thus his victims were allowed to see Benzien as a flawed and abject human being. In this manner, these victims were also able to see that there was a human face to the seemingly all powerful, monolithic apartheid state. If only symbolically, therefore, perpetrators were placed in a situation in which they were exposed to some of the experiences their victims had undergone. This invitation to empathy for the victim, albeit enforced and perhaps only a semblance of the real emotion, was nevertheless an important element in enabling some victims to release some of the intense anger they harboured toward the perpetrator, as a prelude to becoming more open to the possibilities of forgiveness. For in the perception of the perpetrator as a fallible and flawed human being, the victim's capacity to accept that the human condition is a flawed one is fostered; with this recognition, victims' ability to experience forgiveness is promoted.

Apology from the perpetrator

In a related vein, the expression of remorse may evoke forgiveness in individuals who have been deeply injured. While forgiveness should not be made conditional on the perpetrator's repentance as this would, in a sense, leave the victim dependent on the perpetrator, contrition in the perpetrator would be a key factor in facilitating the experience and expression of forgiveness in the victim. This is reflected in the response of one victim: 'I would forgive them if they would come forward. I would be satisfied, because I do not know who did this to me. If I knew the people who did these things to me, I would be satisfied' (Chubb and Van Dijk 2001: 86). As is evident from this, the apparent refusal by the perpetrator to acknowledge his or her actions leads to a lack of closure for the victim and in fact may be experienced as the trauma being perpetuated.

Two other moving events during the life of the TRC are particularly illustrative of the inextricable link between forgiveness in the victim and remorse in the perpetrator. These are the well publicised reactions of the mothers of the 'Gugulethu 7' (seven youths from the township of Gugulethu who had been brutally murdered by the police), and of the parents of Amy Biehl (a young American Fulbright scholar who had been attacked and killed by several youths who were part of a crowd returning from a political meeting in which anti-white feelings had been stirred up).

The responses of the mothers of the Gugulethu youths highlights several complex elements in the forgiveness equation. The question of forgiveness was foregrounded when one of the policemen involved in the killing of the youths sought a meeting with the mothers in which he expressed deep remorse for his actions. Initially most of them rejected his overture, until Cynthia Ngewu unexpectedly and poignantly declared to the policeman that she forgave him. Her willingness to reach out to him effected a dramatic change in the mood of the other women, who spontaneously decided to allow him to redeem himself with them. Rituals for his reintegration within the community were then proposed.

This incident illustrates several elements. First, we would argue that the (initial) unwillingness of the women to forgive was a legitimate response and an authentic expression of the state of their feelings at that moment. To have persuaded them to speak or act in ways contrary to this (e.g. by exhortations to them to forgive) would, in disqualifying their inevitable and appropriate feelings of anger, have been a further act of violence against them. However, the remarkable capacity to transcend her deep loss shown by Cynthia Ngewu was clearly a catalyst that had a transmuting effect on the feelings of her companions. She was able to guide them further along a path of healing through the capacity to forgive that she was able to access within herself. This example indicates that remorse may not necessarily elicit forgiveness, but may sometimes do so. It also suggests that the genuine expression of anger may be a prelude to forgiveness, if the conditions facilitate this. It is also clear from this example that the moral credibility of the individual who advocates forgiveness may be a central factor in evoking forgiveness in others.

The incident of Amy Biehl highlighted another dimension of the forgiveness-remorse conundrum. The response of Amy Biehl's parents to their daughter's murder captured the public imagination. Not only did they choose to forgive the youths who had been identified as their daughter's killers, but they also established community projects in the township in which these youths lived. Their reaction was considered especially remarkable in view of the apparent absence of remorse in the youths concerned. However, subsequent to their interventions, the youth who had struck the fatal blows spoke of his remorse for having killed Amy. This instance suggests that the contrition of the perpetrator may sometimes follow the proffering of forgiveness by the victim, and thus is not always in the anticipated direction (Power 1994). The aspect further highlighted by this example is the possibility of experiencing forgiveness even in the absence of remorse being shown. However, a caveat must be noted that, while this form of forgiveness is valuable when it occurs, care should be taken not to present this option in ways that may be experienced as a demand on those who have been already traumatised. To argue that forgiveness is possible in the absence of remorse being evident or an apology forthcoming is not to say that forgiveness is unconditional. Forgiveness is necessarily conditional, as it is predicated on the expectation and understanding that the offence will not be repeated. To argue otherwise would be equivalent to advocating a form of martyrdom/masochism. In general, it is our view that forgiveness should ideally be linked to a public apology based on an acknowledgment of having injured the victim.

In the context of political trauma, this view of forgiveness may be described as a type of social contract. Forgiveness is thus offered on the basis that there is a guarantee that the atrocity will not recur. This implies a tacit contract, in social terms, where the victim forgives the perpetrator on the clear, if perhaps unspoken, expectation that the perpetrator will not inflict such trauma again.

A religious/ideological framework

Some victims have indicated that if the perpetrator is experiencing some form of hardship in his or her current life situation, they feel able to forgive them even in the absence of an apology or expression of remorse. In this situation, victims appear to refer to a form of divine or higher order justice that has humbled the perpetrator. However, even when the perpetrator continues to hold a relatively powerful or affluent position (and fails to show any form of repentance), victims appear to resolve their frustration at this perceived injustice in the following terms. They state that the perpetrator is ultimately accountable to God and would have to live with his or her uneasy conscience. In some instances, victims assert that the moral superiority of the liberation movements and the oppressed people is once again demonstrated by their comparative magnanimity. This is based on the argument that their willingness to forgive is a further expression of their commitment to the national good, and a denial of their claim to some form of retribution against perpetrators, in the interests of peaceful coexistence.

This recourse to a religious/ideological framework is an especially clear indication of the way in which those from deeply religious backgrounds draw on their value systems to inspire and sustain them in their internal struggle to forgive perpetrators. This serves both as a strength and a weakness in individuals' efforts to forgive those responsible for the trauma they suffered, as will be indicated in the discussion that follows.

Many individuals involved in South Africa's liberation struggle were drawn from the Church (Bishop Tutu is the most prominent example of this) and were steeped in a culture that promoted the notion of forgiveness. It is thus not surprising that forgiveness is often seen in religious terms, and victims experience a strong internal pressure to forgive their former enemies. As previously noted, this predisposition can help some individuals to find meaning and achieve a measure of resolution that might otherwise elude them. In other instances, however, the personal injunction to forgive may add to the internal conflict individuals experience. They may feel guilty in relation to the anger evoked by the experience of being emotionally and/or physically violated and may attempt to disavow these 'negative' feelings in order to forgive those who have wronged them. Since it is difficult to resist the pressure to forgive when one's personal value system provides a moral imperative to do so (but one's emotional state necessitates fuller acknowledgment and expression of more vengeful feelings), the individual may prematurely foreclose on the question of forgiveness. In these instances, forgiveness may be a form of denial, rather than a healthy disengagement from a sense of injury.

Identification with role models (e.g. Tutu, Mandela)

In South Africa, victims were encouraged by idealised parent figures such as Mandela and Tutu (particularly in his capacity as chairperson of the TRC) to forgive their former oppressors. This was often repeated by other powerful figures in the society, so that forgiveness was associated with greater social affirmation. Thus, victims tended to be perceived as more noble if they expressed forgiveness. The implicit communication was that forgiving their former enemies would gain their leaders' approval and would also contribute to individuals' personal healing. The immediate reward for victims was that of blessings, rather than any material gain. However, while the adjurations to forgive clearly fulfilled a valuable social role and also indicated a desirable objective for individuals, it is useful to analyse the function of forgiveness on a more personal level.

The readiness of some victims to respond to the calls to forgive may stem from a deep psychic need for the restoration of a belief in idealised objects. Given that some leaders who are now in positions of power may have been implicated in some of the human rights violations in the Quotro camps (i.e. ANC camps in which suspected spies or informers were incarcerated), the act of forgiveness may have served both a conscious and an unconscious end. One unconscious function served may be that of holding onto an idealised image of particular leaders. This therefore raises the question of whether such forgiveness comes out of a mature position, or an infantilised one.

In this regard, an analogy may be drawn with that of an individual who might offer forgiveness to another in order to elicit or receive the approval of an authority figure. Thus, the forgiveness may be motivated (consciously or unconsciously) by the need for 'parental' approval, rather than resulting from an internal shift. A problem with forgiveness based on this premise is that it sets up some measure of expectation of reward from the idealised parent. If this is not forthcoming, the individual may experience considerable resentment or bitterness, and possibly displaced aggression due to the perceived lack of recognition of the compromise made. In political terms, this could take the form of alienation from the organisation to which the individual was aligned (e.g. this may be evident in the responses of some ex-combatants to their ANC leaders). Thus, forgiveness that is motivated primarily by an impulse to gain the approval of parental figures may be regressive as it has the potential for disillusionment rather than transcendence.

In general, this manifestation of forgiveness tends to be more tenuous in nature (compared to forgiveness which follows a deeper personal engagement with feelings of anger and disappointment, among other feelings). Moreover, in situations where individuals are preoccupied with the external expectations to forgive, there is a potential risk that the trauma they suffered may be exacerbated. Thus, individuals may find themselves caught in a dilemma, where their sense of outrage and anger toward the perpetrator(s) continues to feel authentic, despite the exhortations to forgive expressed by peers and/or leaders they respect. Consequently, any suggestion that they forgive the perpetrator(s) is experienced as being at best insensitive and at worst as a form of secondary traumatisation.

Self-forgiveness

This chapter has thus far been concerned mainly with our observations on the struggles with forgiveness that victims, both those
with whom we worked directly and those who made submissions to
the TRC, were engaged in. At this juncture, it seems apposite
to complement this with more personal reflections on our own
experiences of grappling with issues of forgiveness. As therapists
working with victims of political trauma in the South African
context, and vicariously sharing their struggles to forgive those
who had injured them, we pondered the issues raised for us. In
particular, since our positions necessarily have been informed by
our experiences as black and as white therapists, and given that the
markers of race and class have been especially salient in the South
African context, we believe that some reflection on the implications
of these aspects for us would be pertinent.

In this regard, two of the authors (Straker and Eagle) of the
current chapter have noted the special meaning for them of
working as white therapists in South Africa. They identified the
emotions of shame, guilt and fear as a legacy of living in South
Africa for whites even if they were involved in anti-apartheid
activities. The following excerpt from a paper by Straker (2001)
captures the complexity of their experience:

> Firstly, one has to acknowledge the existence within ourselves
> of the positions of victim/perpetrator, and beneficiary, to know
> that they constellate within us, and then explore them in some
> depth, including the affects and emotions associated with
> them. Despite involvement in anti-apartheid movements, I
> would still describe the state of mind that we experienced both
> then, through the apartheid years, and now, as one which was
> contaminated by shame through association with the apartheid
> state, and driven by self-rejection and guilt at not doing
> enough when others were giving up their lives. In the apartheid
> years we were shadowed by fear, because even that little which
> we were doing, could bring upon us the full power of the State,
> because in South Africa, one was confronted with the use of
> power without limit or constraint. However, currently the real
> issue to be grappled with for me seems to be self forgiveness. I
> need to come to terms with the fact that what I did was enough
> even though it felt insignificant at the time. I also need to move

beyond guilt that I had advantages when others were unfairly deprived. This movement beyond is required, not because the guilt is unjustified but because its indulgence does not allow one to move forward constructively into the future. The question to be addressed now is not where did I fail, but what did I learn and how can this be applied to my own healing and potential contribution to society in the future.

In contrast to the foregoing account, which reflects the experience of a white South African therapist, the first author would wish to articulate her experience as a black therapist as follows. As a black therapist who has worked with victims of political trauma in South Africa, I believe that it may be useful to offer some personal reflections on forgiveness in this context. In doing so, I will use the responses of shame, guilt and fear identified by Straker as points of reference.

As a black therapist, my responses to the issues of forgiveness seem both simpler and more complex than those expressed by my white colleagues/counterparts. They are simpler because my self-identification as a victim of apartheid makes my identification with other victims (the majority of whom were black) of state repression more straightforward. Like them, I too have numerous apartheid related experiences of blighted hopes and assaults on the human spirit to forgive. I feel freer of the burden of shame through associations of race alluded to by Straker, and my engagement with victims' difficulties is thus relatively less complicated.

However, some measure of guilt is sometimes a feature of my engagement with victims, and derives from a sense of the relative insignificance of my personal contribution to the resistance against apartheid. This feeling of guilt is not specific to work with either black or white victims *per se*, but rather is akin to the guilt of the bystander. That this feeling may be shared by many black South Africans who, notwithstanding their opposition to apartheid, were not actively persecuted (e.g. through being detained and subject to torture), is suggested by the following submission to the TRC's youth hearings:

In a moving and surprising submission to the TRC Amnesty Committee, a group of young black South Africans applied for amnesty for apathy. In their application they argued 'that we as individuals can and should be held accountable by history for our lack of necessary action in times of crisis, that none of us did all of what we could have done to make a difference in the anti-apartheid struggle, that in exercising apathy rather than commitment we allowed others to sacrifice their lives for the sake of our freedom and an increase in the standard of living.'

(Chubb and Van Dijk 2001: 215)

Implicit in this apology was a need for individuals to forgive themselves for having failed to make greater sacrifices for their values and ideals.

As this example suggests, the issue of relative privilege (and possible class differences) further complicates the issue of forgiveness. As a black professional, I am aware of the relatively greater degree of material comfort and status I have than is accorded many victims with whom I work. I am also aware that, given this differential, to advocate forgiveness without due thought to what would best serve the individual would be irresponsible. Victims may offer the legitimate challenge that it is easy to encourage forgiveness when one is in a privileged position to do so. In examining and undefensively owning my position as one that is more advantaged than that of many victims, I am more open to the possibilities forgiveness may offer. Thus, I would be able to facilitate a working through of anger and a movement toward forgiveness in victims through a conviction that this is indeed in the interests of their optimal healing. Equally, I can recognise that victims of political violence should be seen as having a choice analogous to that of victims of sexual/physical abuse. As has been noted (Safer 1999), it may not be functional for victims of abuse to forgive the perpetrator in the short term, but rather to use the anger they feel as a source of energy which could provide the momentum for them to free themselves from a state of traumatic bondage. Similarly, victims of political trauma could be impelled by their anger to insist on delivery in terms of the reparations they had been led to expect would be forthcoming. Notwithstanding this qualification, however, I would reiterate that being able to forgive is ultimately liberating for victims. Just as political liberation has been achieved, it is incumbent on the new political dispensation to foster the external conditions that facilitate the work of forgiveness, so that the burden of effort does not reside solely in the individual victim.

Conclusion

During periods of hiatus in conflict zones, or in the immediate aftermath of civil and political battle, individuals and nations are confronted with the challenging question of forgiveness. This issue may be presented by forces internal to them (i.e. they may experience personal pressure to integrate the behaviour and actions which contradict their self-image or changed situation). Alternatively they may be subject to pressure, implicit or explicit, from groups or entities external to them, which are invested in promoting reconciliation in the wider society (e.g. as is considered by many to be implicit in the functioning of the TRC in South Africa). Thus, when the external struggle is no longer prominent, the internal struggle is foregrounded.

In the light of this, the question of forgiveness has a particular poignancy for victims of political trauma. They are called on to exchange their previous involvement in external forms of struggle (i.e. through their role in the liberation struggle) for an engagement in the more internal psychic struggle of forgiveness. Thus, even as the liberation movements to which they belonged succeed in overthrowing their oppressors, it becomes evident that the cause for which they fought requires further sacrifices of them.

However, many victims engaged with the issue of forgiveness in ways that were consistent with its empowering nature. Perhaps in recognition that forgiveness is potentially a potent force, it may be wielded by victims almost as a weapon, so that a refusal to forgive functions as a weapon.

Despite this possibility, it must be acknowledged that this weapon may be a double-edged sword, as it could be mutually destructive (i.e. take a toll both on the individual who wields the power not to forgive, and the perpetrator who remains unforgiven). Hence the refusal to forgive has costs for the person. The choice and capacity to forgive the perpetrator is ultimately freeing for the victim. If she or he is able to forgive, the victim becomes less preoccupied with the reason she or he was damaged, which is an important milestone on the road to trauma recovery.

References

Chubb, K. and Van Dijk, L. (2001) *Between Anger and Hope: South Africa's Youth and the Truth and Reconciliation Commission.* Johannesburg: Witwatersrand University Press.

Doyle, G. (1999) Forgiveness as an intrapsychic process, *Psychotherapy*, 36(2): 100–8.

Fow, N. (1996) The phenomenology of forgiveness and reconciliation, *Journal of Phenomenological Psychology*, 27(2): 219–33.

Freedman, S. and Enright, R. (1996) Forgiveness as an intervention goal with incest survivors, *Journal of Consulting and Clinical Psychology*, 64(5): 983–92.

Hamber, B. and Wilson, R. (1999) Symbolic closure through memory, reparation and revenge in post-conflict societies. Paper presented at the Traumatic Stress in South Africa Conference, hosted by the Centre for the Study of Violence and Reconciliation in association with the African Society for Traumatic Stress Studies, Johannesburg, 27–9 January 1999.

Mamdani, M. (2001) A diminished truth, in W. James and L. Van De Vijver, *After the TRC: Reflections on Truth and Reconciliation in South Africa*. Athens, OH: Ohio University Press.

Orr, W. (2000) *From Biko to Basson*. Johannesburg: Contra Press.

Power, F. (1994) Commentary, *Human Development*, 37(2): 81–5.

Safer, J. (1999) *Forgiving and not Forgiving*. New York: Quill.

Sells, J. and Hargrave, T. (1998) Forgiveness: a review of the theoretical and empirical literature, *Journal of Family Therapy*, 20: 21–36.

Straker, G. (2001) The dream of reconciliation: the reality of fragmentation. Paper presented at the Psychotherapy and Reconciliation Conference, Sydney, February 2001.

Tutu, D. (1999) *No Future without Forgiveness*. New York: Doubleday.

Chapter 8

My journey towards wholeness and forgiveness with the aid of therapy

Joy Green

> Everyone says forgiveness is a lovely idea, until they have something to forgive.
>
> (Lewis 1996)

At 50, after working for 30 years in children's homes, I started a social work training course and found myself in a place of fear and depression, questioning my abilities. My self-esteem plummeted and my Christian faith, somehow, became less fulfilling and available to me. Psychotherapy started me on an unexpected journey to self-discovery and ultimately forgiveness. In this chapter I will offer my journey in order to encourage others to find what is hidden within their lives and to give therapists an understanding of the complexity of any process towards forgiveness.

Background

My father was an officer in the air force, and spent more time overseas than at home. I have a brother two years younger than me. Because of the war, he was 3 years old before he met my father for the first time. My grandmother lived with us, so we were raised by her and my mother. My mother was a powerful woman who ruled us with a rod of iron. I seemed to take the brunt of her wrath. I don't really remember much affection being shown but I do remember the cane kept at the side of the kitchen cupboard. My grandmother shared my bedroom. She was a gentle soul who said very little and did not argue with my mother. My father retired from the services when I was 14, and it was only then that I really got to know him. We had a great time together. He died of cancer when I was 25. I deeply regret the years I missed being with him.

What I do remember of my childhood is school, activities at church, writing weekly letters to my father and all the goodbyes when he left after holidays or weekends. Church played an important part in my life, even as a child. We would go to church three times on Sundays. I would be entered for scripture exams and elocution and singing competitions organised by the church. But I did miss out on fun. I was never allowed to collect the prizes I won, nor receive presents on my birthdays. We were not even allowed to play outside with other children.

I went to work in a children's home, and, over the next three decades, mainly cared for young children who had been abused or had multiple disabilities. As a matron for 17 years, I was used to carrying responsibility. I saw my work as a practical expression of my Christian faith and as where God wanted me to be. I found it challenging, fulfilling, and it was my life! I enjoy being with people and believe I was seen as compassionate, sensitive, fair and with a sense of humour. I have patience and fought injustices faced by children in a responsible and professional way. I was known for this and gained respect. I had been brought up not to show anger as this was not Christian. The emphasis was on loving your enemies and forgiveness. I had to struggle with this as my role was also to care for the parents who had abused their children and I would have liked to have seen them suffer the full consequences of their actions. I worked hard and all hours but towards the end, having given so much of myself to so many, I had little more to give and was almost burnt out.

After the death of my mother, I started to think about my future and the path I would take. To move on, I needed further training and I was accepted on a social work course. But I was exhausted and I found it difficult doing the course at the same time as coping with the loss of both caring for the children and my mother. I knew I had to do it for my own satisfaction and career development: I thought of it as a chance to stand back from all the pressures, look objectively at my life and work, find out 'who am I in all of this?' and move on. However, it produced new challenges and suddenly things I would normally have handled capably provoked different responses which I could not understand. I particularly remember becoming upset in a seminar discussion talking about child abuse. I had spent years attending court for the most horrendous cases and caring for children who had suffered serious consequences of abuse. I had experienced little emotion and saw it very much as part of my professional life and work. Suddenly the feelings were overwhelming.

Therapy was suggested by a college tutor whom I trusted. Although I had no idea what this would involve, I agreed to consider it but made the stipulation that I work with a Christian therapist whom I hoped would understand where I was coming from and why certain aspects of belief were so important to me. She suggested someone and after meeting together and feeling reasonably comfortable with her, we agreed to begin the journey.

Therapy

I had buried so much of my past to enable me to lead a relatively happy and fulfilled life and was, certainly, not aware of anything I needed to forgive or let go. It was only in the course of time that I became aware of how affected I was by what had happened to me. I had no idea what therapy would entail and thought it would be a short journey, more of an excursion. But, what started as an excursion ended up as a long haul lasting a total of five years.

To have company

I knew there would be common ground as the therapist was a Christian. But she was not of the same denomination and I recognised we would not have exactly the same beliefs. I didn't know my companion and had to test the relationship and build up trust. This was not easy for me. I had been very independent and in control of my life and now, unusually for me, I was on the receiving, not the giving, end of being helped. I was aware there were three of us on this journey: God, myself and the therapist. The therapist and I needed to be open to God and seek His guidance and help.

But my faith was also a barrier to the therapy. I had to trust someone else other than, or as well as, God. I felt guilty and an enormous sense of failure as a Christian that I needed to ask for help. There was also a sense of shame, so much so that I felt unable to tell people that I was in therapy, for fear of their reaction. The

Church gives out ambivalent messages about therapy. This was highlighted in an address given by the Archbishop of Canterbury in Amsterdam (July 2000) where he said 'When therapy replaces faith and when therapeutic techniques are seen as the total answer to humanity's deepest needs and longings, another idolatry is introduced'. This is an example of the suspicion felt by many Church representatives and it perhaps prevents a number of Christians having therapy.

I guess I was very unsure of what I was getting myself into and a little battle went on as I was testing out how skilled my therapist was and whether I could trust her. I was determined not to use the tissues provided! I had built up a defensive wall to protect myself and to conform to the type of person people wanted me to be. Poor therapist!

To experience

Very gently a relationship developed. I found difficulty in working out the therapeutic role. She felt like a friend, but she was being paid to work with me and was causing me pain. There was a great deal of talking and, gradually, we achieved an understanding of each other and started to explore one thing after another as they revealed themselves. As I grappled with feelings of devastation, I knew that in my own strength I could not deal with them alone. I remember drawing a picture of all the loads I was carrying. They felt like heavy boulders breaking my back. That is when I found the comfort and strength of a loving God who gave me the ability to hold on and face what I did not want to hear.

A few months into therapy, I remember saying I had had a happy childhood. 'Did you?' I was asked. The tears came and I needed those tissues. Suddenly I was held and felt safe. She did not laugh and I didn't have to pretend to be strong any more. We argued, cajoled, prayed, talked and I became angry at what I was finding out. I dreaded the sessions, yet counted the days to our next meeting. No one had ever really listened to me before and I found there was much I had repressed.

There were strange feelings of vulnerability and yet dependency on the therapist. I began again to question what I was doing. Was it right to delve into the past? Why was my faith not strong enough to enable me to deal with these issues? I had always been the person who people turned to, and now the roles were reversed. The loneliest period of my life was spent experiencing the events which had formed my personality. What was hardest was the pain.

Tears flowed like rivers and I cried myself to sleep most nights. I was exhausted, had difficulty in getting through each day and yet I was holding down a job where people depended on me. I had a reactive depression and needed medication for a few months, as a holding situation, while we uncovered more and more painful experiences. These had been buried very deeply and had never been shared, and now there was some sense of relief that at last someone was actually making time to listen to me, and that I mattered. I worried my therapist would give up on me, despite assurances she wouldn't. I expressed my anger in tears. She showed no signs of judgement, only acceptance and compassion. Yet I assumed the opposite and transferred these feelings to the therapist who often had to say 'I am not your mother'. It probably took a good year before I could believe this.

Gradually we removed layers of the onion skin, starting with the easiest, and working to the core. 'Easiest' was thinking about my brother, the favoured child, 'mother's boy', now with three failed marriages behind him. I had taken on my usual carer role when his first wife was dying of cancer. I became guardian to his two teenage children, then aged 16 and 15, as my brother was overseas. He stayed abroad, leaving me to care for them and deal with situations he could not handle. I was now becoming aware of my anger which had turned to resentment.

Another layer of the onion was to do with my father. I was so proud of him and, as I wrote earlier, the happiest times in my childhood were when he was at home and I felt safe and protected. Yet there were so many years when he was away. My therapist suggested he could have left the services earlier, he could have chosen to be with the family, particularly me. I was so angry with her and refused to acknowledge he had made this choice. For the first few years of therapy, I could not hear anything against him.

It was two years into therapy before I could face my memories of an incident with two men when I was 9 years old. I had always had a distant memory of where and what had happened. I needed psychotherapy to allow myself to admit that I had been raped and nearly murdered. For 40 years it had been my secret – my mother died not knowing. I had told no one because of my belief that, as a Christian, sex was not something I should talk about. I went into a state of shock and denial as I unearthed the atrocity. It began to make sense why I had always had difficulties relating to men. On the social work course, I felt bullied by my tutor who had negative views about Christianity and challenged me on my sexuality. I felt devastated – and angry, because here I was being taught about anti-discriminatory practice and yet I was being discriminated against. And I felt powerless to challenge her, as I feared she would try to fail me and I had too much to lose.

But it was my mother who was hardest to face. She had always represented to me the epitome of Christianity. Yet, in the course of therapy, I became aware how different she was from the image I had carried. During one therapy session, I somehow feared she could hear me talking about her – and she had been dead for five years. I did not want to say anything bad against her. But I came to accept that her love was conditional and I never did meet her expectations. She was very controlling. She always said, without my father around, she had to be father and mother, so needed to be the disciplinarian. The hardest thing for me was to acknowledge that she had let me down.

I began to admit to myself and my therapist that there were times when I was both physically and sexually abused by her. As a young child, I shared a room with my grandmother. When I was 12 my grandmother had a stroke and I moved out of the bedroom and shared a bed with my mother for some months. She would inappropriately touch me and I would often pretend I was asleep to try to stop it happening. With hindsight, I realise that I was being used to meet her needs, though I didn't recognise this at the time. But at the same time, sex was never discussed. I got the message that sex was dirty and it was men who were not to be trusted. Yet here she was sexually abusing me. And if she felt I had been really naughty, she would hit me either with a garden cane or a news-paper rolled up very tightly. I remember the pain.

I managed to leave home at 17 and began to build a life apart from her. But at 25 I was back, spending all my spare time sup-porting my mother after my father's death. When she developed cancer, she came to live with me for ten years until her death.

What I am describing are so many issues around anger, loss and wasted opportunity. I had tried to be there for everyone: my mother, sister-in-law, niece and nephew, and, over the years, the children in the homes, but I had been unable to be there for myself – unable to face my own grief.

To move

Decisions had to be made. I could stay in this horrible dark tunnel, with the darkness of depression which Seamands (1995) so aptly calls 'frozen anger', with resentment which was causing me physical as well as the emotional problems, or I could move on. I did not know where to begin and I certainly didn't think I had the resources. At this time I was struggling with my faith and kept asking 'Where are you God?' I wanted to give up therapy – I couldn't take any more, but I knew I couldn't stay like this either.

This was my lowest point on the journey, but it was also a turning point. I knew that however weak my faith was at that time, I had to hold on to God's promises and get my help from Him. I reassured myself that the therapist had been trustworthy so far. I acknowledged I needed help and I decided to stay. I felt like I was starting a new part of the therapeutic journey. Talking about my past was difficult enough, but to do something about it felt even harder! I can see how much easier it is to feel the victim than to move forward, make choices and change.

There was a battle of wills between myself and my therapist, particularly when she tried to convince me that to move on with my Christian beliefs I had to forgive. I thought I had long since forgiven, but in reality I hadn't. I had just buried the hurt deeper and deeper over the years. I believe forgiveness takes a real effort and is particularly hard with people who are important to you. To forgive, I believe, I had to change the way I had always responded to people and circumstances. But I needed to learn how.

I read books, went to Christian meetings and a healing retreat where I met other Christians who had come through their own difficulties and shone. I gained hope and encouragement. My therapist encouraged me to use this alongside the work we were doing. I had desperately wanted to succeed with my social work training as I had had a bad experience at grammar school. I did well on the course and began to feel a little better about myself. But I knew I was holding onto too much, and I had to *let go and let God.*

After my social work training, I went to visit friends in Australia. They are very special people who I knew would accept me as I was and to whom I didn't have to pretend. They were the first people I confided in about my journey into the unknown. It was important to me to share what was happening with someone other than my therapist and feel supported. They were particularly helpful as they knew my parents, so what I was saying was real to them and to me. They did not say therapy was a waste of time and money. What a relief! I had never seen so many sheep before. I felt as though I had been shorn with lots of cuts on the way and yet as Jesus said, 'I am the Good Shepherd, I know my sheep and my sheep know me' (John 10:14).

I had a wonderful journey, but running away didn't take away the pain and nor did medication. My therapist had told me it was necessary to feel the pain and anger, understand what had happened to me, in order to be able to move on. I decided to give up the medication. All I could do now was to pray, 'Help me God' and continue to trust my therapist that I could move on from this. I found my therapist's long holidays were a particularly difficult time. I kept a journal so I could write down what I was feeling, instead of bottling up everything until she returned. Most important, I had to hold onto the belief that I was making a journey in the light of God.

To learn

I had to learn to trust people and I had a few close Christian friends who supported me through this time. Where once I felt I was the only person who had ever gone through such pain, I met other people who were making similar, painful journeys. I began to feel hope.

In putting the jigsaw together, I recognised that I had grown up being controlled and conforming. With my mother, I always tried to earn her love, but it was never quite good enough. I had taken responsibility for the mess my brother was making of his life. With the abusers, not only was there an abuse of power, but I had lost my sexuality and was left with fear. Living and working on the job, I had allowed myself to be totally taken over, believing this level of responsibility was required of a professional and a Christian. Within my church I was brought up in the fear of God, and that you had to earn His love. I was taught 'love your neighbour as you love yourself', but I didn't love myself. I lacked self-esteem and had great difficulty in receiving – why would people want to give to me? I felt unloved and unlovable.

No wonder I was always tired. I was working so hard at trying to please everyone, and earning their respect, that there was little time for me. As well as this being a time of learning, in therapy it had to be a time of unlearning – all the mechanisms I had used to exist needed to be broken so I could be the person God wanted me to be, start to love and enjoy being me without feeling controlled.

To discover

Forgiveness is at the heart of the Christian faith. We forgive with our head all the time, with minor hurts and let downs, but forgiving from the heart is something quite different. As Christians, we pray 'forgive us our sins, as we forgive those who sin against us', yet it can be so hard to do. In my journal, I kept writing 'I want to let go, but I can't!' However much I tried to forgive, I failed as I was trying to do it with my own strength. I needed God's grace, the undeserved love of God, to achieve this. I believe that we have to draw near to the cross of Christ to understand true forgiveness. An unforgiving heart grieves God. I kept asking 'Who am I?' without getting an answer, but I had to accept that I would only find out in God's good time.

I started to realise it was all right to be real, that I didn't have to pretend. It was all right for people to see my hurt as well as my joy. A dear friend, with a very special ministry, was praying with me one day. She said God had given her a picture of me being likened to a chrysalis and I would emerge as a butterfly. This gave me hope. Not long after this, I had a dream of me sleeping peacefully in someone's hands. When I looked further the hands had holes in them. I knew it was Jesus himself. I drew what I had seen and for the first time felt God was showing me how loved I was and that I was safe in His hands. This was the turning point for me in my journey and in my faith, and the drawing continues to be very precious to me. I was totally at peace with myself. I experienced God's love in a very new way. There was nothing to fear. He was the Father I didn't have. I was adopted into the family of God and I didn't have to earn His love.

As I felt more and more loved by God, it became easier to let go of the things that had bound me tight. I saw the need to forgive the deep hurts that people had caused me, so that I could move on from this place. I feel that forgiveness is ongoing, and the Holy Spirit shows what is needed. With the people I needed to forgive, it happened in different ways.

To forgiveness

With considerable emotional effort, I wrote to my brother, in a loving and unaggressive way, explaining the hurts he had caused me. He said he was sorry, but he has gone on causing pain and I now recognise that he lacks insight into what he does to people. I am aware I still need to work at forgiving him and accepting him as he is. But I no longer take responsibility for him so, in that way, he has no hold over me. I feel sorry for the mess he is making of his life and trust he will find some happiness.

I have forgiven my mother in different ways and at different times – and received a lot of prayer support in order to do this. At a Mother's Day service in church I was helped by recognising the pain other people feel towards their mothers. People who felt hurt were invited to go to the cross and put a tulip there in memory of their mother. I found myself remembering the time when a friend had advised me to write down the biggest hurts on a piece of paper. I did this and, without sharing it, burnt the paper. To me, this was symbolic of letting go of the hurts and I prayed that God would take away the pain. The tulips I saw others place at the foot of the cross were like the list I had burnt. It seemed so appropriate to give these hurts to God and leave them there in the form of a flower. About half of the church went forward and the pain could be felt all around. In the afternoon I became very upset and recognised my own pain was still there and there was more to forgive. So very quietly and on my own I did this.

One of the last things I did in therapy was to tear up a letter from my mother which I had opened just after her death. In the letter she had reminded me what good friends we had been and said what a lovely daughter I was. I had become increasingly aware that this was what she wanted me to believe. Destroying the letter was so hard, as it was one of the few mementos I had left of her. But I knew I had to do it in order to be free of half truths and false impressions. I can also now say that my mother loved me as best as she could, but she had her own needs and issues.

I recognise that forgiveness can be an ongoing thing. As different memories come to mind, it is possible to deal with them as they arise without it being necessary to go back to therapy. What I learned in therapy was that I can be in control and I now have the resources within me to forgive and let go of the feelings.

Although I felt there was nothing to forgive my father for, in therapy I recognised some years later that I did need to forgive him for not being there when I needed him – other things, especially the abuse, might have been avoided. I met my tutor some years after I left college, when the power balance had shifted. I was able to talk to her and quietly recognised she had a problem and I was able to forgive her. The pain has gone. As for the abusers, I at first said I could never forgive them. After my dream I described above, with the promise of God's love for me, I knew I had to forgive and pray for them. I felt it was right to return to the place where it had happened. My therapist agreed to come with me – I don't think I could have done it on my own. I felt I was reliving the awful experience. The pain was overwhelming. I felt I had gone into shock and had difficulty talking. The later outcome was that there was a change, but I still felt I really hadn't let go. I had a trusted friend return with me a few weeks later. We did a prayer walk together, starting at the church, and we retraced the steps I had taken on that awful night. We prayed *en route*, for me and for the men. I felt I really had now let go and was free of that event. I can talk about it now, no longer feel a victim, but a survivor.

I felt I had to forgive the church in which I had grown up. In those days God was to be held in awe and there was a feeling that you had to earn His love. With the help of my therapist, I had moved on to experience a joy and freedom in worship. I changed my church to one where I felt I could experience God in a new and personal way and was baptised as an outward sign of my new life.

Concluding words

It is interesting to note that in the deaf sign language, the sign for forgiveness is wiping the palm of one hand firmly across the other, as if removing any stain or mess that clings to it. In retrospect, I think that forgiveness, for me, was the stage before letting go, before I was able to remove the mess that clung to me. In writing this chapter, I have been surprised by how hard it has been to remember the process. This has been reassuring, as it seems symbolic of the fact I have been able to forgive and let go.

To the question 'Who am I?', I recognise that my past is part of my present, but with God's help it is possible to change, leave the bad things behind and look forward in hope. God protected me on my journey, and through my darkest times. I learnt never to underestimate the power of prayer and that my tears were not wasted, they were all part of the healing process. As a Christian, I had never before felt worthy to wear a cross around my neck and I now wear the cross with pride. With God as my driver and my therapist as my travelling companion on this journey, I had reached my destination and felt able to face life again, but in a new way. *En route*, I have met some remarkable people who have become my friends, and see them all as God given to me.

I discovered therapy is not a sign of weakness, but an indication of strength, that there are treasures in the darkness, which had seemed to be out of reach. I saw God's hand at work in choosing the right therapist for me. One who became a trusted friend, who was skilled in her work and wise in her counsel. She accepted me as I was and walked the lonely path beside me. I feel loved and loveable and I know I am forgiven and have the ability to forgive others. Five years on, there is no turning back, and I am enjoying my life, and feel able to let go and let God.

Henri Nouwen in *The Path of Peace* (1995: 40–1) writes,

> Where is this peace to be found? The answer is clear. In weakness. First of all in our own weakness, in those places in our hearts where we feel the most broken, most insecure, most in agony, most afraid. Why there? Because there, our familiar ways of controlling our world are being stripped away. There, we are called to let go from doing much, thinking much, and relying on our own self-sufficiency. Right there where we are weakest, the peace that is not of this world is hidden.

References

Lewis, C.S. (1996) *Mere Christianity*. New York: Touchstone Books.

Nouwen, H. (1995) *The Path of Peace*. New York: Crossroads/Herder & Herder.

Seamands, D.A. (1995) *If Only*. Buckinghamshire: Scripture Press.

Chapter 9

Letting go: a question of forgiveness?

Cynthia Ransley and Terri Spy

The editors set off on an exploration of forgiveness – two people with very different views on the subject. We were aware of the paucity of material written in the UK and the range of research and literature coming out of the USA, largely emanating from psychologists with a belief in the value of forgiveness.

We brought together writers – psychotherapists, counsellors, social workers, a criminologist – with expertise in working in particular areas of practice. We hoped they would offer different perspectives on how people let go of wrongs and hurts and discuss the extent to which they saw this as linking with forgiveness.

Some of the authors gave a personal view of the term forgiveness. Several wrote from a belief in its positive power. They saw it as freeing the victim from a preoccupation with the wrongdoing and the offender, and as ultimately, in Moosa, Eagle and Straker's words 'a milestone on the road to recovery'. Two expressed misgivings about the term itself. And a warning was given about the potential misuse of power, in the sense of people feeling coerced (because of their religious, cultural or political background) to forgive, or of forgiveness being bestowed from a place of superiority.

Ransley's research (Chapter 3) suggests that the word forgiveness is not as widely used as terms such as letting go, acceptance and becoming reconciled. These latter terms may be useful, in our more secular society, as they do not carry religious overtones. However, they are imprecise. 'Letting go' may emanate from a place of unforgiveness or disinterest in the offender. Equally the person using the term may equate it with forgiveness. However, we must also be aware, as Ransley pointed out in Chapter 1, that people give very different meanings to terms such as forgiveness. In this book, authors tended to emphasise three different aspects to forgiveness:

- an intersubjective process involving the full participation of both partners, actively sought and welcomed by both (Cooper and Gilbert, Chapter 4);
- the choice to give the gift of letting go and redirecting energies away from grudges (Carroll, Chapter 5);
- (the giving) up of resentment to which a person has the right and the giving of the gift of compassion to which the offender has no right (Moosa, Straker and Eagle, Chapter 7).

Forgiveness in the last two definitions is seen as offering a 'gift'. Carroll's words acknowledge the gift of letting go of grudges while Moosa, Eagle and Straker's definition also involves offering compassion to the offender. There is a strong argument that the defining quality of forgiveness is its sense of being a gift based on, as the philosopher North (Enright and North 1998) puts it, the offering of 'moral love'. This links straight back into the ethical and religious roots of the term. We argue that letting go of resentment and the offering of compassion can be seen as different levels of forgiveness.

What makes it possible to offer this gift? Much of the American literature (see Chapter 1) focuses on the importance of the victim developing empathy and understanding for the wrongdoer and on the victim making a conscious decision to forgive. To some extent, both are echoed in the chapters of Spy and Green (Chapters 2 and 8). Their notion of forgiveness comes from their Christian tradition – that in order to be part of the Kingdom of God, they must forgive as they are forgiven by God. The onus, therefore, is upon the victim forgiving, rather than forgiveness depending on any action from the wrongdoer. We are unclear about the extent to which the Christian message underpins the American thinking. Very likely, it reflects the individualistic culture of the USA – an encouragement to move away from a narcissistic preoccupation with the self.

What is interesting is that *none* of the other chapters in this book come out of this individualistic perspective. They explore what might be called a relational model of forgiveness or letting go. They focus on the offender's role in helping the victim survive the process. In a sense, they explore what the offender must do so that the 'gift' becomes less undeserving.

This is clearest in Cooper and Gilbert (Chapter 4). Figure 4.1 (see page 76) offers the reader a two-way process model of forgiveness in working with couples. In fact, their model can be applied to the other settings explored in the book. For Carroll (Chapter 5), from the standpoint of an institution, forgiveness is also seen as a two-way process. He offers a model for the mediator, in which the organisation accounts for the wrong done, offers reparations or sets up procedures so that it does not happen again.

Masters (Chapter 6), from a criminal justice perspective, looks at the way restorative justice seeks to help victims move on – the word forgiveness is deliberately excluded – through meeting the offender. For some victims the opportunity to tell their stories is sufficient. Others find comfort in meeting with the offender. Ideally, the onus is on the offender taking responsibility for his or her wrongdoing by way of apology, explanation and possibly reparation. Finally, within the South African political arena, Moosa, Straker and Eagle's discussion of forgiveness (Chapter 7) is placed within the context of the Truth and Reconciliation Commission (TRC) which laid the onus on offenders to acknowledge and confess their wrongdoings.

In these terms, letting go of bitterness and hurt becomes less a question of forgiveness than a response to the offender (hopefully) taking responsibility, apologising and offering reparation in front of a witness. Ideally the wrongdoer offers empathy and compassion to the victim (a focal shift from much of the American literature we have discussed). Forgiveness, in terms of compassion and the dropping of hostilities, may (possibly) emanate from this. This is nearer, in terms of religious roots, the Jewish tradition discussed in Chapter 1.

The process of helping the victim move on is within a *relational context* which involves the offender, the practitioner and, as is set out so clearly in Chapter 7, the cultural and political context – the community. For Spy and Green, the cultural and relational context involves their Christian community and God. In this wider context, we need to pay heed to the person's relative power or powerlessness in their relationships and in society.

Disenfranchised wrongs

There is no suggestion that it becomes easy for the victim to let go of his or her hurt and bitterness – forgive, if you will – just because the offender is willing to meet and to fully admit their guilt. It may continue to be hard, even where the offender shows willingness to listen and offer empathy and compassion. However, unwillingness to acknowledge wrongdoing adds to the trauma. Even worse are situations where victims are not believed by their family or community and the wrong becomes disenfranchised. The victim becomes increasingly out of relationship, not just with the offender, but with other close relationships and the community. This inevitably affects the support available and the sense of shared meanings and roots. And there is an increased internal disruption to his or her sense of self and personal identity.

Often clients seek help because they are not in a relationship and are having to face a wrongdoing with very limited, if any, support. The offender may be unwilling to meet them, he or she may be dead. Any work with individuals who have been traumatised by a wrongdoing must respect their cultural and sociopolitical context, and, in many ways, this is symbolised by the debate over forgiveness. Any framework therapists use for thinking about their work must allow for the client for whom forgiveness is a concept dear to his or her cultural beliefs. It equally needs to respect the variety of beliefs others hold.

Our view is that the process of coming to terms with a wrongdoing involves loss and mourning, with a particular focus on the betrayal, or wrong done, by the other. This will deeply impact the person's sense of safety in the world. Our thinking has been influenced by Thompson's (2002) useful critique of traditional models of loss and grief, Kubler-Ross' (1969) thinking on death and dying, Worden's tasks in the grieving process (1991), Herman (2001) on trauma and Kepner's healing tasks with adult survivors of abuse (1995).

Mindful of our differences, the co-editors have together developed a model for working with individuals which can encompass forgiveness and non-forgiveness. The dual orientation model comes out of Stroebe and Schut's 'dual process approach to loss' (in Thompson 2002). They view grief reactions as involving two processes or 'orientations' which take place at the same time. They write of 'the grief orientation' and the 'restoration orientation'. The grief orientation holds the responses we might anticipate in loss and mourning such as panic, sadness, anger and shock. The restoration orientation describes the attempt, right from the beginning, to find ways of managing the loss and moving forward. Their description of the oscillation – moving one way and the other, back and forth – underpins our model (see Figure 9.1).

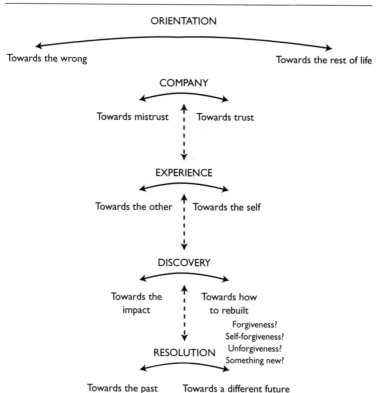

Figure 9.1 The dual orientation model

Within the overall orientation – towards the wrong and towards the rest of life – there are four tasks. We use the word task to avoid any notion that there is a neat and tidy pathway in the process of rebuilding – 'complete this stage and you will move on to the next'. Tasks can be undertaken in different orders. Any task will only be partially addressed at any one time, and individuals move back and forth between them.

Central to the model is empathy. We see as primary the offering of empathic attunement to the individual who was wronged and helping the person develop empathy and compassion for him or herself. From this place, individuals may begin to understand and feel compassion for (forgive, if you will) the offender. But this is their decision. The individual in Herman's (2001) words must be 'author' of his or her recovery and the work based on empowerment.

The dual orientation model

At first, the primary orientation is likely to be to the wrong, going over and over what happened, telling and retelling the story. However, from the beginning there is some orientation to the rest of life – for example, physical self-care, caring for dependent others, even making plans for the future. Where the shock or response to the trauma is great, the person may need others to take over even the basic needs of providing food and warmth for a period. On the other hand, the response may be to dissociate or attempt to shut out what happened by *only* focusing on the rest of life. The individual needs to be able to oscillate between the wrong and the rest of life. As time goes on, there is, hopefully, an increasing orientation towards the rest of life, though the pull to the wrong is always there. At any one time, one will be figural and the other in the background.

Within the overall frame, the four tasks in the healing process each involve an oscillation between two orientations. The tasks 'company', 'experience' and 'discovery' were named by Green, in the previous chapter, as points in her personal therapeutic journey. For Green, the endpoint was forgiveness. We have called it 'resolution', to allow for forgiveness being one, rather than the only, goal.

Company

Given the disruption being wronged has on the sense of self and relationships, Green's notion of company, as the first task in the process of recovery, is apt. There is a need for company when bonds have been disrupted. Herman (2001) describes the creation of new connections as a core need in recovery. But there are clearly particular challenges in developing feelings of trust and safety when you have been wronged. Therefore within company there is an oscillation between the orientation to trust (this time it's going to work, I'm going to be really safe here, I can really depend on her) and the orientation to mistrust (relationships never work, that therapist is no good, I'll never manage it, it's all too frightening). The person needs to develop a balance, a sense of trust which is mindful of safety.

Green wrote primarily of the struggle to make contact and feel safe in a therapeutic relationship. But there may be a need to help the person develop self-support/self-care and feelings of safety in his or her own company in order to embark on the difficult journey of facing betrayal, and to understand whether there is external support available from family, community or faith beliefs.

Green's therapeutic journey involved herself, God and the therapist. She showed how crucial it was that the therapist empathised with this. Moosa, Eagle and Straker (Chapter 7) showed the need to tune into the impact of the client's community, the social, political and cultural context.

At this point, on occasions, the client may identify a goal of, or concerns around, forgiveness. The therapist may find it useful to consider what the client means by the term. Is there a link with faith or cultural beliefs? Does the person feel under any pressure to forgive? Is looking to forgiveness acting as a defence against the pain? Does the client have a sense of how forgiveness might be reached? Of course, the client may be using other language for the goal such as wanting to let go of resentment, accept, become reconciled. The same questions apply.

There will be a need, in Worden's terms (1991) to 'actualise' the wrongdoing, begin the process of sharing the detail in order to make the story more real. What happened? How did it happen? Who was to blame? Where the transgression was in childhood (especially early childhood) there will be particular difficulties here and we commend readers to Kepner's work (1995) on psychotherapy with adult survivors of childhood abuse.

Experience

The tension between facing the feelings and the fear of doing this may well provoke a return to the previous task and the need to renegotiate trust and safety in the therapeutic relationship, and strengthen self (and possibly) community support.

Within experience, there will be an orientation towards facing feelings related to the wrongdoer – anger, hate, vengeance, empathy – and an orientation towards facing feelings about (or in relation to) the self and the loss – pain, guilt, anger, shame and self-blame.

People who have been wronged need to experience the range of feelings, and will oscillate between feelings towards themselves and feelings towards the wrongdoer. There is cause for concern where the person is only able to face one of the orientations. Feelings of hate, anger and thoughts of revenge are a reasonable response to being wronged and feeling powerless. But a person can get stuck alternating between the past (the wrongdoing) and a fantasised future where vengeance will be done or justice will prevail. This may come to serve as a defence against the enormity of the loss. On the other hand, people often turn the wrong towards themselves and become deeply distressed, overwhelmed by guilt and self-punishing. This is especially the case when they have been partly responsible. They find it hard to look out and identify the guilt of the other. We need to be mindful that there may be cultural or familial introjects governing what are seen as acceptable feelings.

There is a need to experience and re-experience the range of feelings and hopefully begin to mourn the loss and, for some, mourn giving up the hope of revenge. For many this will be difficult, particularly where the wrongdoer denies they were responsible or the perpetrator cannot be identified.

Discovery

In discovery there is an orientation towards how to rebuild and, with this, the inevitable orientation back to the impact of the loss and injustice. The impact may well feel so negative (the death of a loved one, the end of a relationship, the trauma after abuse) that the person tips back into re-experiencing painful feelings. Note the circular nature of any response to a wrong or loss. People may be discovering what impact the injustice has had on their lives. What or who have they lost? What's the impact on self-esteem? Have relationships changed with others? Have roles changed in the community? Do they have some responsibility for what went wrong?

Coping with a traumatic transgression or loss inevitably brings a crisis in meaning, a crisis in the individual's half-conscious assumptions about the world. Long-held faith or spiritual beliefs may be questioned. There is an urgent need to reconstruct meaning. Davis and Nolen-Hoeksema (1998) suggest the first aspect is to try to make sense of, find some kind of explanation for, the wrongdoing. This underpins much of the searching – going over and over the story, contacting the authorities, fighting for justice, confronting the offender. Paradoxically, what is involved in the searching is also part of the rebuilding. What choices are available? What steps need to be taken? How can I support myself? Who can help? How can I stop feeling so guilty?

Where the person continues to be consumed by bitterness and finds it hard to let go, Spy raises the question of forgiveness – asking clients to consider what it would be like to forgive and how that compares with their current unforgivingness. (She would check whether the words fit with the clients' use of language.) Ransley has reservations about the therapist being so specific and has some concerns that the suggestion may be experienced as a criticism or might slant the direction of the client's path. Spy believes that raising one direction – forgiveness – is a way of opening the discussion. Ransley is more drawn to Kepner's (1995: 143) view that 'we must be careful not to project our own beliefs and needs – religious, scientific, or political – onto the client instead of joining in an *experiential investigation* of what would be correct for that survivor': what would help them in the healing process?

Whatever the therapist's practice, the survivor is (hopefully) discovering a way of reorientating towards the wrong and the wrongdoer. For many, the issue of self-forgiveness will be important. The person may begin to make the decision to forgive. Or they may be questioning whether, in Safer's (1990) terms, 'moral unforgiveness' is more appropriate – taking a stand to oppose the injustice, to tell the truth. As she puts it, the client must be the 'author' of their recovery. Ransley believes the healing may involve no active decision. In the oscillation back and forth between rebuilding and facing the impact of the wrong, between facing the feelings about the other and grieving for the self, attitudes towards the other may imperceptibly change. In Galdston's words (in Durham 2000: 78) 'the blocking introject loses its significance. The goal of revenge passes'. Galdston calls this forgiveness. Ransley suggests, sometimes, this may simply be letting go.

Resolution

In resolution the oscillation will continue. There is an orientation towards the past but also an orientation towards a different future, one where, as Kepner puts it, the survivor reorientates to what has happened as being past, 'an aspect, not the whole of her nature' (1995: 144). And we need to acknowledge that some do not reach this point.

At a time when people are having to find new ways of being in the world, there is a continued quest to reconstruct meaning, to find a narrative thread which links who they were before the wrong and who they are now. We have written of the need to make sense of what happened. Davis and Nolen-Hoeksema (1998) identify a second need in reconstructing meaning – to find some benefit from what has happened. When the wrong has been traumatic, such as the death of a loved one, it can feel disloyal to admit that any good has come from it. Davis and Nolen-Hoeksema's research showed that where people could find some benefit (spiritual, existential, practical) they made a more successful adjustment. It may be the satisfaction of setting up a self-help group, bringing a wrongdoer to justice, finding new spiritual beliefs or living life in the present. And finding a benefit must be centred on the awareness that there are some things that cannot be changed, that we can only do so much. For some, this is an impossible task – the loss is too great.

Reconstruction of meaning after a loss or transgression involves two complementary movements: to conserve what was viable before the loss and to construct a different being in the world when this fails. There is a need, as Neimeyer and Anderson (2002) put it so well to 'relearn the self' and 'relearn the world'. Part of the relearning is finding a place for the past – developing a continuing narrative which integrates what has happened and yet is open to what the future will bring.

Spy and Ransley have different views on resolution. Ransley has some discomfort with the word itself, nervous that it sounds too simple, too final, too complete. Spy sees forgiveness as a resolution. It may be a lengthy process to achieve this, but she believes that once forgiveness has been reached there is both resolution and peace. Both place emphasis on the sense of process. However, Ransley is uncertain whether, in the face of a major trauma, the resolution is ever 'complete'. Her sense is of a self that is always evolving and of an existential quest which has a never-ending quality.

Conclusion

We started this journey with different views on forgiveness. As we end it, we are aware that this is based both on our different belief systems and a different view of the self. We are both committed to helping people move on from a life consumed by bitterness and hurt. We both have a belief in the value of human relationships and the need to transcend wrongdoings if we are to avoid the never-ending cycle of retaliation. In the end, what matters is not whether letting go of a wrong is a question of forgiveness, it's having the capacity to break out of a destructive cycle, to find our unique path to healing and the courage to face a different future.

References

Davis, C.G. and Nolen-Hoeksema, S. (1998) Making sense of loss and benefiting from the experience: two construals of meaning, *Journal of Personality and Social Psychology*, 75(2): 561–74.

Durham, M.S. (2000) *The Therapist's Encounters with Revenge and Forgiveness*. London: Jessica Kingsley.

Enright, R.D. and North, J. (1998) *Exploring Forgiveness*. Madison, WI: University of Wisconsin Press.

Herman, J.L. (2001) *Trauma and Recovery*. London: Pandora.

Kepner, J.I. (1995) *Healing Tasks*. San Francisco: Jossey-Bass.

Kubler-Ross, E. (1969) *On Death and Dying*. New York: Macmillan.

Neimeyer, R.A. and Anderson, A. (2002) Meaning reconstruction theory, in N. Thompson (ed.) *Loss and Grief*. Basingstoke: Palgrave.

Safer, J. (1990) Must you forgive?, *Psychology Today*, July/August.

Thompson, N. (ed.) (2002) *Loss and Grief*. Basingstoke: Palgrave.

Worden, W. (1991) *Grief Counselling and Grief Therapy*, 2nd edn. London: Routledge.

Index

186   Index